That Job He's Got to Do

From the author of

Buy the Truth and Sell it Not:
The Life of E. Gaston Collins

William Lafayette Cook

That Job He's Got to Do

The Life and Times of William Lafayette Cook

Frank N. Cook

Unclouded Press
Lewisburg, Tennessee, USA

ISBN 978 0 9912785 3 4 (Library binding)

ISBN 978 0 9912785 4 1 (Softcover)

Library of Congress Control Number: 2017910717

Library of Congress Subject Headings:

Reelfoot Lake Region (Tenn.)--History.
Tennessee--Race relations.
Honor--Southern States.
Earthquakes--Missouri--New Madrid.
Violence--Reelfoot Lake Region--History--20th century.

BISAC Subject Headings:

BIO002000 BIOGRAPHY & AUTOBIOGRAPHY / Cultural Heritage

HIS036120 HISTORY / United States / State & Local / South

SOC018000 SOCIAL SCIENCE / Men's Studies

BIC Subject Category: BGH

Thema Subject Category: DNBH Biography: General: Historical

Cover Art: Cypress trees near Blue Bank, Reelfoot Lake

Published in Tennessee, the greenest state in the land of the free, in the United States of America. Printing location is indicated on the final page of this publication.

WARNING: This work of non-fiction describes a time when the only triggers that caused men concern were attached to firearms pointed in their direction. Modern gentle souls who are emotionally triggered by frank discussions of race, violence, and cultural deprivation should read with caution.

In Memory of Woodrow Francis "Woody" Cook (1941-2012): fisherman, duck hunter, guide, bull rider, graduate of the University of Memphis, Federal Wildlife Resources employee, husband, and father, whose chance conversation set the author on a journey.

Contents

Preface

William Lafayette Cook was something of an enigma. He was the grandfather I never knew, and yet I *know* him. I know the lives of the children he produced. I know something of the times in which he lived. I know myself.

Many people have helped to fill in some of the gaps. A list of some of those people may be found in the acknowledgements following this work. Much supposition and self-reflection have also gone into the study. If this work is not faithful to the life and principles of Will Cook, it is the author's fault entirely.

We cannot live in the past. What has gone before neither increases nor diminishes us. We can either allow our lives to be dragged down by what has happened in the past, or we can learn from those who came before and thereby elevate our lives. "Lives of great men all remind us, we can make our lives sublime, and departing, leave behind us, footprints on the sands of time."

- F.N.C.

Society never advances. It recedes as fast on one side as it gains on the other.

It undergoes continual changes; it is barbarous, it is civilized, it is christianized, it is rich, it is scientific; but this change is not amelioration.

For every thing that is given, something is taken. Society acquires new arts, and loses old instincts.

— Emerson, *Self-Reliance*

That Job He's Got to Do

Black Jack Hollow, Reelfoot Lake
Courtesey of Dr. Robert E. Clendenin, Jr.

1.
A Beautiful Place

It goes past the powers of my pen to try to describe Reelfoot Lake for you so that you, reading this, will get the picture of it in your mind as I have it in mine. For Reelfoot
Lake is like no other lake that I know anything about. It is
an afterthought of Creation.

– Irvin S. Cobb, *Fishhead*

The Great Master's garden, beauty fit for a King, a place of
romance, a wonderland of mystery, a sportsman's paradise, a
bird-watcher's delight, a photographer's joy, a woodcraftsman's
dream, a comfort for the soul, the world's greatest natural fish
hatchery, the scientist's outdoor laboratory, and the Mecca of all
good hunters and fishermen – these are all phrases used to
describe Reelfoot Lake.

The lake and surrounding area became a popular destination
for outdoorsmen soon after it formed in 1812. John James
Audubon killed a bald eagle twenty miles southwest of Reelfoot at
Little Prairie Bend in 1820. He illustrated this eagle in his famous
book *Birds of America*.[1]

Bald Eagle by John James Audubon

Chapter One

In 1821, David Crockett rode to the Rutherford Fork of the Obion River thirty miles southeast of Reelfoot to view 800 acres he had purchased. It didn't take him long to find the hunting much to his liking. During seven months in the winter of 1825-1826, Crockett claimed 105 bears killed in the area.[2] Another settler, Reuben Edmonston, claimed eighty-nine bears one year.[3]

Col. Crockett's Desperate Fight with the Great Bear.

Word of the natural bounty soon spread to Carroll County, Tennessee, seventy miles to the southeast. One resident there, R.S. Cole, described many hunting and fishing trips to Reelfoot that he began making in 1832.[4] Carroll County was also home to two brothers who would eventually come to Reelfoot, John and Will Cook.

**White Crappie,
courtesy of John E. Phillips**

By the mid-nineteenth century, Reelfoot provided a living for many hunters and fisherman. J.C. Burdick arrived at Reelfoot in 1876, buying and selling fish in the Walnut Log area and later moving to the Samburg area.[5] In Memphis, Tennessee, Wm. Yanakay & Co. of Beale Street and Victor D. Fuchs of Jefferson Street advertised Reelfoot Lake fish for sale. Signaigo's of Beale Street advertised Reelfoot perch, red snapper, and white fish.[6] By the 1920's, the Kelley Fish Company of Lexington, Kentucky was advertising black bass, newlights (crappie), bream, and dressed catfish from Reelfoot Lake.[7]

Susie Stretches,
courtesy of Trey Richardson

An 1880 Memphis newspaper advertised ducks from Reelfoot. Canvas-backs sold for a dollar a head, mallards for seventy-five cents a pair, teal for sixty cents per pair, and wood or butter ducks for fifty cents per pair.[8] At one time swans were an abundant species at Reelfoot. Their meat was considered a delicacy, and their feathers were prized for ladies' hats and quill pens. They were shipped to Nashville and Memphis by the boxcar load and sold for twenty-five cents each.[9] Swans were hunted to extinction locally and did not come to Reelfoot for many years. Thankfully, they were reintroduced into the area and are gradually making a comeback.[10]

Canvasbacks   Wood Ducks

Another Reelfoot animal sold for food was the snapping turtle. "Imagine a creature with moss-covered shell, thick as armor plate, as big as a washtub ... with huge feet bearing heavy claws ... snapping its powerful jaws, hissing and leaping at curious tormentors, and you have a picture of this denizen of the dismal swamps."[11]

The abundance of the game at Reelfoot was matched by the beauty of the surroundings. An 1874 visitor said, "From the marshy shore spreads out the vast extent of the seemingly level carpet of vegetation – a mat of plants, studded over with a host of beautiful flowers; through this green prairie runs a maze of water-ways, some just wide enough for a pirogue, some widening into pools of darkened water. All over this expanse rise the trunks of gigantic cypresses, shorn of all their limbs, and left like great obelisks, scattered so thickly that the distance is lost in the forest of spires. Some are whitened and some blackened by decay and fire; many rise to a hundred feet or more above the lake."[12]

**Reelfoot Lake stumps by Donald V. Sabin,
with permission of Tennessee State Library and Archives**

A New York magazine of 1876 described many features of Reelfoot Lake, including Grassy Point, Long Point, Horse Island, Starved (sic) Island, Choctaw Island, and Blue Basin, which it said was of unknown depth.[13] (There was a common belief at the time that Blue Basin was bottomless.) A Louisiana newspaper in 1890 said, "Reelfoot Lake presents the appearance, all times of the year, of a thickly studded turnip patch. The growth known as bonnets, broad leaves floating on the surface attached to stems which are often many feet long springing from the bottom of the lake, give one the impression from the shore that he is looking upon an immense field of solid soil, yet thousands of skiffs, especially in winter, skim the surface. The rasping of the keel over the bonnets sounds like sandpapering a wooden instrument."[14]

**Cypress and spatterdock (mule foot) near Grassy Island, Reelfoot Lake.
Lotus also grows throughout the lake.**

In 1891, the New York Times described a trip to Reelfoot: "Far out in the lake, beyond the sight of shore, one gets the impression of being in a vast ruined temple. On every side rise endless spires of decaying cypresses, branchless, leafless, shorn of their beauty, gleaming in the still air like gaunt, mysterious monuments of destruction and death."[15] Tennessee Senator Edward Ward Carmack called Reelfoot "The Great Master's garden of weird, fantastic beauties, nature's maze and labyrinth of never-ending wonders."[16]

A 1910 writer spoke of "the moss-covered bottom ... millions of fish ... cypress knees ... lilypads ... bass, crappie, and sun-fish ... the 'honk' of wild geese ... feeding ground of mule foot, jonqua-pin, or smartweed ... long-necked birds, cormorants or watertur-keys ... a great fisheagle ... (and) a king fisher, hammering away, trying to kill a skip jack he has just captured."[17]

Ducklings near Gooch's Landing, Reelfoot Lake.

When Albert Ganier first visited Reelfoot in 1915, he had missed the major migration but still counted fifty-nine species of birds.[18] It is believed today that over 240 species of birds inhabit or visit the area and that fifty-six species of fish swim the waters. A million ducks and geese spend time there each year.[19] A 1915 writer called Reelfoot the world's greatest natural fish hatchery, and modern scientists agree that it is an extremely great natural fish hatchery.[20]

A *Field and Stream* writer in 1927 remembered the "mighty splash of a sleepy, hundred-pound catfish disturbed; the tall giant skeletons of age-old cypress trees against the livid western sky; the water about us blood-red in reflections."[21]

Sunset at Kirby Pocket, Reelfoot Lake.

In 1938, local writer Cecil Humphreys listed the most numerous ducks at Reelfoot as mallards, pintails, redheads, black duck, and teal. The game included beaver, otter, raccoon, opossum, mink, muskrat, and squirrel. The largest fish, he said, was the alligator gar, which reached eight feet long. The spoonbill catfish also grew large and along with crappie were very popular.[22] The 25,000 acres of open water, cypress swamps, bottomland forests, sloughs, marshes, and mudflats nurture creatures of every sort. Part of the area became a National Wildlife Refuge in 1941.

There are numerous suggestions for the origin of the name Reelfoot. One incorrect assertion is that it wasn't named until March 18, 1839, when a man with a deformed foot who was called Reelfoot Jones drowned in Spring Creek, causing the name to be changed to Reelfoot Creek.[23] Some have suggested the name of the lake comes from the resemblance of the lake's outline to a misshapen foot or to a staggering gait. Some suggested it was from the frequent quakes which caused people to reel when they walked. An African-American tall tale *Luster and the Devil* says that a big man named Luster dug all the way to Hell trying to get his feet warm and the resulting lake was named in honor of his feet.[24]

Bayou de Chein, courtesy of Dr. Robert E. Clendenin, Jr.

The lake's name actually originated in September of 1785. When the North Carolina surveyor Henry Rutherford found a small Indian settlement near Bayou de Chein, he christened a nearby river Reelfoot after the Indian chief.[25] Some say the chief's name was *Red Foot*, but a transcription error later changed it to Reelfoot.[26]

| "Red Foot" map | "Reel Foot" map | "Reelfoot" map |

Several faux Indian legends have grown up about the lake. The 1910 *Legend of Reelfoot Lake* is very similar to a more popular 1929 tale, except that it featured Moccasin instead of Chickasaw Indians. The 1926 tale, *Yellow Butterfly Summer*, credited Manitou, the Great Spirit, with creating the lake he called Laughing Waters so the Mandan people would always have food and clothing. The most popular of the faux legends, the 1929 *Legend of Kalopin,* suggests that a Chickasaw Indian Chief (who was named Reelfoot because of his deformed foot) drowned when the lake formed and gave the lake his name.[27]

The only authentic Indian legend about the creation of Reelfoot involves Tecumseh, the chief who tried to unite all Indian tribes so they could defeat the white man. When Tecumseh could not convince a Creek tribe to join his alliance, he angrily told them that he would return home. He said that when he reached Detroit, he would stamp his feet. This stamping, Tecumseh said, would shake down every house in the Creek village. The Creeks began counting the days after Tecumseh left. By their reckoning, he would reach Detroit on December 16, 1811. Early in the morning of December 16, the Creek village was destroyed by the New Madrid quake, or if you believe the legend, by Tecumseh.[28]

Today Reelfoot Lake remains a popular destination for fishing, hunting, and recreation. It has been said that "if you ever taste Lake County water, you will always come back."[29] One modern sportsman spoke for many when he said, "Once upon a time a loving God touched His finger to earth and created a spot as close to Heaven as there is, and it was named Reelfoot Lake."[30]

Moonrise over Upper Blue Basin

The Great Earthquake at New Madrid

2.
A Violent Place

You've come from nowhere, but now you're headed for Hell.
- a Kentucky settler to some travelers bound for Reelfoot

Reelfoot Lake was born in a cataclysm of nature's violence. Earthquakes of magnitude 8.0 and greater are not common. On average only one per year occurs somewhere in the world. In the area where Arkansas, Missouri, and Tennessee come together, five of these massive quakes, along with thousands of smaller shocks, struck within a space of two months.

At a quarter after two o'clock in the morning on December 16, 1811, there was an estimated 8.6 quake centered in Blytheville, Arkansas.[1] In Louisville, Kentucky, 280 miles to the northeast, people rushed into the streets, certain that the world was coming to an end.[2] Chimneys collapsed in Cincinnati, Ohio.[3] In Columbia, Tennessee, 190 miles to the southeast, people endured ten to fifteen minutes of shaking accompanied by a peculiar sound and followed by a large cloud of black smoke passing overhead.[4] Two hundred miles to the east, at Rock Island, Tennessee, great blocks of sandstone crashed down a mountain.[5] In Washington D.C., 900 miles to the northeast, President James Madison was awakened by the shaking.[6]

That same morning saw two more earthquakes in the same area, with an 8.0 centered in Steele, Missouri, at 8 a.m., and an 8.0 centered in Little Prairie, Missouri, at 11 a.m. On that day two towns disappeared: Little Prairie, Missouri, and Big Prairie, Arkansas.

Clearing the River

Chapter Two

On the Mississippi River, miles of banks caved into the river, and many boats were seen no more. Two islands disappeared. The earth heaved and cracked open in great fissures, spewing out sand, smoke, and water.

Aftershocks continued until January 23, 1812, when an 8.4 quake centered at Portageville, Missouri, struck at nine o'clock that morning. Like the December 16 quakes, this one was felt over much of the country, from the Rocky Mountains to the East Coast, and from Canada to Mexico. In Boston, twelve hundred miles to the northeast, the ground swayed enough to ring church bells. Just east of the Mississippi River in Tennessee, there were several sloughs and channels which held water from the December 16 upheaval. Some creeks were also dammed up by sand boiling from the ground. Two weeks later, all of these would combine with the falling landscape and inrushing river to form Reelfoot Lake.

Mississippi River upper left, Reelfoot Lake lower right

West of the Mississippi River, so much sand boiled out of the ground that today there remains 136 acres of sand near Deering, Missouri, that locals refer to as "the Beach." Traces of sand can be seen today in fields all over the area.

That Job He's Got to Do

Many aftershocks continued until the morning of February 7, 1812, when the largest of the New Madrid quakes and the second-largest earthquake in American history occurred.[7] At a quarter after three o'clock in the morning, there was an 8.8 earthquake centered in Marston, Missouri, just southwest of New Madrid. The river erupted with waterspouts and whirlpools. Huge waves of water were thrown onto the surrounding land. Some boats were stranded on the land. Many other boats disappeared.

An uplift of land called the Tiptonville Dome was created between Reelfoot Lake and the Mississippi River. It measures about 9 miles by 7 miles and is now called the Lake County Uplift. The Mississippi River ran backwards from the Island 10 area toward the north for at least several hours. Water poured into the depression that became Reelfoot Lake. Two low waterfalls and rapids were created in the river at the Island 10 area and also across from New Madrid. These persisted for two or three days until the river wore them down.

Lake County Uplift outlined in red

Chapter Two

In the next month, on March 26, 1812, a major earthquake occurred in Caracas, Venezuela, in which 15,000 to 20,000 people were killed. The U.S Congress authorized a payment of $50,000 for five shiploads of flour to be sent for aid. No aid was immediately forthcoming for the self-reliant people of the New Madrid area.

Three years later, Congress did pass the first disaster relief act in U.S. history, the New Madrid Relief Act of 1815. This authorized the granting of new land to settlers whose land had been destroyed in the quake, but the majority of people who profited from the act were speculators and fraudsters. Of the 516 land certificates issued, only 20 went to original New Madrid area landowners.[8]

The aftermath of the New Madrid earthquakes found some of the land impassable with large fissures running across it. Travelers often feared the land would collapse into a hidden chasm. Aftershocks continued for many years and caused the area to be known as "land of the shakes."

The area continues to be an active seismic zone. Tiny tremors are so common that they are hardly noticed.[9] The largest quakes since 1812 have been one of 6.6 magnitude in 1895 centered in Charleston, Missouri, and one of 5.4 magnitude in 1968 centered in Dale, Illinois.[10]

The swampy conditions created by the flooding of Reelfoot made a haven for snakes, including cottonmouths. Boaters were often afraid that snakes would drop from an overhanging tree into the boat. One settler said the land had fifty bushels of frogs per acre and enough snakes to fence the whole property.

It is not clear how many settlers and river travelers lost their lives in the New Madrid earthquakes. It is even less clear how many Indians were killed. Despite the sparse population, it is quite possible that many, many people lost their lives in the quakes.

Besides suffering physical harm, many Indian tribes were also affected psychologically. Tecumseh and some other chiefs had been urging Indian tribes to band together and kill all white men, so that the land would once again be theirs. Tecumseh had prophesied that the land would belong to the Indians until the Great Water (the Mississippi) ran backwards. When the Mississippi actually did run backwards during the quake, many tribes felt it was a sign that the Indian no longer had a chance of defeating the white man.[11]

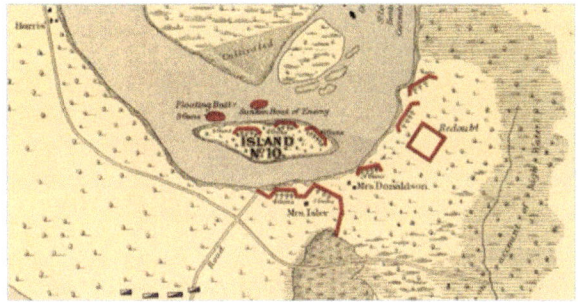

Confederate positions on Island 10 and riverbank.

Fifty years after the river ran backwards, more violence came to the Island 10 area when the Union Navy used the Mississippi River to invade the South. The Confederates had fortified Island 10 where the river makes a sharp curve just as it enters Tennessee. They also placed batteries on the bank facing upriver. This thwarted the Union gunboats from February 28 till April 8, 1862. Eventually, boats slipped past under cover of darkness and outflanked the Confederates. This defeat was overshadowed by another Confederate defeat on the same day at Pittsburg Landing, or Shiloh.

Before the Union boats were able to pass Island 10, they had conducted a heavy bombardment of the area. For many years afterward, collectors and farmers continued to find cannonballs left from the battle. In 1937, when the river broke through the levee downstream from Island 10, a 24-pound cannonball was uncovered, another remnant of the Island 10 battle.[12]

Chapter Two

Bombardment and Capture of Island No 10 on the Mississippi River
by Currier & Ives

The defeat of the Confederates by the Union forces did not end violence in the area. For many years afterward, an incident called the Beckham Massacre stayed fresh in the minds of locals. On August 4, 1863, a group of black Union soldiers were rowed from the Island 10 garrison over to the Kentucky Bend shore. From there, they walked three miles to the Frank Beckham farm on the opposite side of the bend. The Beckhams had sixteen slaves, but these troops were looking for one particular slave girl and also for money. When they didn't find either, they first ransacked the house, then killed Mr. Beckham and his father, clubbed to death the oldest daughter, and drowned two other daughters and the baby. These soldiers were court-martialed in Columbus, Ohio. Four were sent to the penitentiary, and six were hung.[13]

Another incidence of violence occurred in the area in 1869, when a group of KKK decided they wanted to disarm the black workers of local planter Willis Jones. Jones had been a strong supporter of the Confederacy, but said his workers were now free and peaceful and should be allowed to have arms. When the gun-control group arrived, Jones and his workers stopped them. Two intruders and three of the workers were killed.[14]

Forty years later, there would come another period of violence that pitted neighbor against neighbor and involved the survival of the lake itself. This, we will later see, was the time of the Reelfoot Lake Night Riders.

Sunrise at Champey Pocket, Reelfoot Lake.

Reelfoot Lake was beautiful but could also be deadly. In June 1928, a group of Boy Scouts died on the lake when they were caught in a sudden thunderstorm. Sudden winter storms could be deadly to hunters and fishermen. More than one sportsman has perished from hypothermia during the winter. More than one swimmer has drowned in the lake. More than one boater has died after striking an underwater stump and capsizing.

Chapter Two

Lake people generally liked and respected each other, unless one intruded on another's territory. A sure way to ask for trouble was to get caught running someone else's trotline. A hunter who built a new blind too close to an existing blind might find that it got struck by lightning on a clear night.

Moonlight
on Reelfoot Lake
The Sportsmans Paradise
Near Lake.City

c
1922

Donald V. Sabin photo, by permission of Tenn. State Library and Archives

The swampy conditions in the area were an incubator for mosquitoes. An 1841 settler noted that the area was "luxuriant in disease and death."[15] When the Yellow Fever epidemics of the 1870's were claiming many lives along the river, some people retreated to safer places in Tennessee, such as Sulphur Springs near Cedar Grove. The mineral waters there were believed to prevent the disease. Sulphur compounds *are* used in disease-fighting sulfa drugs, but no doubt the people benefited the most by getting away from mosquito-infested swamps.

Will Cook's brother John moved from Carroll County to Lake County in 1888. In 1902, a newspaper reported that people in

Carroll County were "stirred up" by a case of smallpox involving Will and John's brother. "The victim is Joe Cook, a young white man who is well known. He contracted the disease in Lake County while visiting his brother, J.N. Cook at Cronanville a short time since. He is now convalescent and will be out shortly."[16] At least 150 cases of smallpox were reported in the Reelfoot area in 1910.[17] Smallpox outbreaks also occurred in 1931 and 1932.[18]

The worldwide flu epidemic struck in the fall of 1918. As late as the 1920's, Lake County had a malaria death-rate twice that of neighboring counties.[19] Floods sometimes contaminated water supplies. Dr. J.P. Moon reported in 1937 that the floods had polluted wells and caused five cases of typhoid fever.[20] Diphtheria outbreaks occurred.[21] Sometimes all dogs in the county had to be quarantined due to rabies outbreaks.[22]

Lake County and Reelfoot Lake were a Heaven on earth for rugged sportsmen and settlers, but for those who fell victim to its dangers, violence, or disease, it could seem to be the opposite eternal destination.

Cypress trees, Reelfoot Lake

Map of northern Lake County, Tennessee

3.
Tennessee's Last Frontier

Go West, young man!
      - John Soule & Horace Greely

Chickasaw and Choctaw Indians controlled West Tennessee in 1818, with the Choctaw living primarily to the south in Mississippi. The ancient Mound Builders of the Reelfoot area were long gone. The Chickasaw had expelled the Shawnee and resisted the incursions of the Iroquois, who were also pressured by westward expansion. Eventually, the Chickasaw realized that they, too, would be overrun by European settlers. On October 19, 1818, Andrew Jackson and Isaac Shelby concluded a treaty with the Chickasaw chiefs ceding all claims in West Tennessee and western Kentucky to the U.S. government.

Once the Jackson Purchase was completed, settlers began pouring into the area. Sportsmen, as we've seen, were drawn to the Reelfoot Lake area, but most settlers wanted good farmland. West Tennessee had lots of that, some of it with large areas that had already been cleared by burning.

Family lore says that the Cook family had been in America for a long time. One ancestor supposedly had a pepper patch in New York City where the Empire State Building now stands.[1] Family lore also says that while Tennessee was being settled, three Cook brothers crossed the mountains from North Carolina into Tennessee. One brother remained in Middle Tennessee. Another traveled west of the Mississippi River. The third brother, Thomas Cook, who was Will Cook's great-grandfather, eventually settled in Carroll County, Tennessee, along with his son Joseph.

Chapter Three

Coming Round the Mountain by John H. R. Pickett

The yoke used on one of the Cook ox-teams

Carroll County, like much of West Tennessee, had fertile soil in a gently rolling landscape, with abundant streams and good timber. There was plenty of wild game including bears, wolves, panthers, wildcats, deer, raccoons, foxes, rabbits, squirrels, quail, doves, and wild turkeys. A few places, known as *barrens*, had sparse timber and poor soil but enough vegetation to make good hunting grounds.

When it was time to build a cabin, a settler would choose an elevated spot of ground close to a good spring. "The timber and shrubbery were cleared away; trees were felled, lopped the desired length, and hauled to the spot; a huge oak was felled and riven into boards. When full preparations were made, a day was fixed and the neighbors for miles around were invited to the raising. Not to be invited on such an occasion was regarded as a grand insult." Once the log walls and roof were in place, "a door, and perhaps a window was cut out; a rude fireplace was constructed, and a chimney built, composed of sticks daubed with mud. Floors were made of slabs split from logs. The settler then turned his attention to clearing and fencing a spot of ground to raise grain for bread."[2]

Pioneer Home on the Western Frontier by **Currier & Ives**

Years later, one Carroll County resident reminisced about his old home place. He fondly remembered "the orchard on the hill; the apples, the peaches, and the pears; the old spout spring, the branch with its minnows so bright, and ducks that played in the water so clear; the old chestnut trees and the poplars so tall, and the sheltering beech that grew by the spring."[3]

The typical pattern of West Tennessee settlers was first to plant corn, and then to raise hogs. This produced the fastest and largest amounts of food for survival. When Thomas Cook died in 1832, his will divided his stock of hogs between his widow Ann and his son Joseph. The family spinning wheel and check reel were left to

Ann. She no doubt could spin fiber into yarn, an important pioneer need.

Typical pioneer spinning wheel

West Tenn. soap making

Once settlers like Thomas Cook had met their basic needs, excess corn, ham, and bacon could be sold for cash. Settlers also planted cash crops such as cotton or tobacco. West Tennessee was prime cotton country. Farmers in West Tennessee produced no cotton in 1818 but seven years later were producing forty thousand bales per year.

Cotton increased the demand for slaves. From 1820 to 1830, the number of slaves in Tennessee increased by sixty thousand, most of those likely going to West Tennessee.[4] Thomas Cook's will left his slave Ben to his widow Ann and son Joseph.

Thomas Cook's son and daughter-in-law, Joseph and Nancy (the grandparents of Will Cook), were moderately successful farmers. Once a settler had lived on unclaimed land for seven years, he could claim it with an occupant grant. In 1847, Joseph Cook used an occupant grant to claim 250 acres near Cedar Grove in southern Carroll County lying southwest of the Rutherford Fork of the Obion River.[5] The 1850 census lists four hundred dollars in real estate to his name. Among other children, Joseph and Nancy had a son, Lawrence Decatur (Dee) Cook, born in 1836.[6]

When Tennessee voted to secede from the Union in June 1861, not all Tennesseans agreed with the decision. Support of secession correlated somewhat with slave ownership but was by no means absolute. Three-fourths of the people who fought for the Confederacy were not slave owners.

Conversely, there were men who accepted slavery but who believed that preserving the Union was a more important issue. By the mid-1800's, the Christian principles upon which America had been founded had already made the USA a beacon of liberty and justice to the world. Many people could not bear the thought of splitting up such a country. Robert Cartmell, a farmer from Jackson, Tennessee, wrote:

> "What a pity! To severely tear up and destroy the best government ever devised by the ingenuity of man or revealed by heaven; except for the slave question, I believe no other question could sever the bands of Union by which we are united. The Union ought to be preserved."[7]

Another West Tennessean expressed it this way, "I give my head and my heart to God and our country – one country, one language, one flag."[8] A group of men in Carroll County (including Dee Cook and his future brother-in-law) also felt this way.[9]

Dee Cook enlisted in the Union Army at Trenton, Tennessee, on November 1, 1862. He joined Company F of the Seventh Tennessee Cavalry. The Civil War has often been called a war that pitted brother against brother, and this was true in the Cook family as well. Dee Cook's older brother George served the Confederacy for four years with the Thirty-second Mississippi Infantry. After the war George lived in Mississippi and then in Keene, Texas, south of Ft. Worth, where he died in 1912.[10]

Chapter Three

Dee Cook's military records show him enlisted, not as Lawrence, but as *Lycurgus* D. Cook. It is possible that this is a transcription error. It is also possible that it shows a tendency for Dee to have fun with his own name at the expense of others. In the 1870 census of Carroll County, Dee is listed as *Lorenzo* D. Cook. Lorenzo Dow was an eccentric backwoods preacher of the early 1800's. Lycurgus was an ancient Greek statesman (showcased in *Plutarch's Lives*) who showed an interest in the common man. Dee Cook was apparently not uneducated.

Dee Cook's military career was short. Enlisting in November, he was one of the seven hundred who were captured the first pop out of the book by Nathan Bedford Forrest at the battle of Trenton in December of 1862.[11] In the custom of the day, they were paroled. They took an oath not to take up arms against the Confederacy anymore until they could be exchanged. They also agreed to make their way to a parole camp, with many of them sent by rail to St. Louis and then on to Ohio.[12] Some reports say that Forrest told the Tennessee boys to go home.[13] Perhaps Dee Cook did go home first, for he is listed by the parole camp as deserted on February 2, 1863. Shortly thereafter, on February 6, he arrived at the parole camp at Camp Chase near Columbus, Ohio. Eventually, he was exchanged and returned to Tennessee, where he mustered out (was honorably discharged) in October 1863.

During the war, Dee served alongside Lafayette and Napoleon McKinney, whose grandparents, James and Elizabeth McKinney were also early settlers of Carroll County. The McKinneys came from South Carolina, along with their son John. John married Francis Edwards, also of South Carolina, in Tennessee in 1842. John and Francis were successful farmers. By the 1870 census, they had six thousand dollars in property and three black servants. Among other children, John and Francis produced a daughter, Francis A. McKinney, born in 1848. Francis' two brothers, Lafayette and Napolean, fought for the Union in the same company as Dee Cook. Napolean did not survive the war, dying of pneumonia at Camp Chase in Ohio. Dee Cook was given fifty acres by his father in January 1864. A year later, he married Francis A. McKinney.

William Lafayette Cook[14] was born to Dee and Francis Cook in Carroll County, Tennessee, Monday, October 26, 1874. Less than a month after Will was born, his grandfather, Joseph Cook, died. A little over two years later, his grandmother, Francis McKinney, died.

When Will was almost six, he and his four sisters and two brothers suffered the worst loss of all.[15] Their mother, Francis Cook, died of tuberculosis at thirty-two years of age. Dee Cook did not remarry, and no doubt his two oldest daughters, Mary (or Mollie) and Nancy, aged fourteen and twelve at the time, took over much of the responsibility of caring for the other children.

The Cedar Grove community where the Cooks lived, as one would expect, was named for a large grove of cedar trees. A store and mule-powered cotton gin were part of the community. A water mill on nearby McCanney Creek provided a place to grind wheat and corn. A Methodist church in the middle of the cedar grove served as a social center and school.

CEDAR GROVE SCHOOL AND METHODIST CHURCH
1897 · J. WESLEY WILLIAMS , TEACHER

Another schoolhouse was built about 1830.[16] It was a one-room building where six grades studied and recited. Furnishings were a teacher's desk, a blackboard, poplar benches, a wood-burning stove, a water bucket, and a dipper. Recess typically found the girls playing jump-rope while the boys played baseball games with homemade balls and bats. School began at eight o'clock and ended at four. The older boys would help the teacher haul a supply of wood after school.

Woodard's School House, Miss Vennie Parson, Teacher, Cedar Grove

Tennessee did not have a compulsory education law until 1913. At that point, children from eight to fourteen were required to attend school eighty days per year. Many farmers did not believe schooling was important for boys. Reading and writing and doing a little ciphering was all the formal education that many boys wanted. Most left school by age sixteen.

The schools in Cedar Grove were subscription schools, which were types of private schools. They were blessed with good teachers who believed in a good foundation for their students. Will could read and write just fine. The two surviving signatures we have from Will show a fine hand, but his middle name is spelled

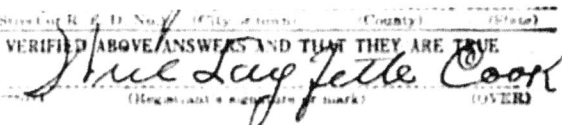

Layfette, the way someone with a southern drawl would pronounce it by elongating the last two syllables of Lafayette into a single drawn-out syllable. Will Cook finished the eighth grade in Carroll County[17] and then went to work on the farm.

The earliest picture we have of Will Cook is a tintype, probably made around the turn of the century when he was in his twenties. County fairs at the time often featured a photography booth where one could get a tintype made.

Will Cook

Will Cook's in-laws, William Alexander and Mary Ellen Hammer were relative latecomers to Carroll County. The 1900 census shows them living in Grainger County, Tennessee, with their six children, including the youngest, Rachel Emma. Six years later, the Hammers were living in Carroll County, where the 18-year-old Rachel Emma married William Lafayette Cook on September 20, 1906.

Will, who was thirty-two when he married, was described as short in stature with medium build, dark hair, and grey eyes.[18] He had been farming with his father since boyhood but apparently didn't see much future in Carroll County, where it was a constant struggle just to eke out an existence. The newlyweds Will and Rachel headed west. Seventy-five miles due west from Cedar Grove was Barr, Tennessee, on the Mississippi River in Lauderdale County. Here Will and Rachel's first child, Eva Pauline Cook, was born August 15, 1907.

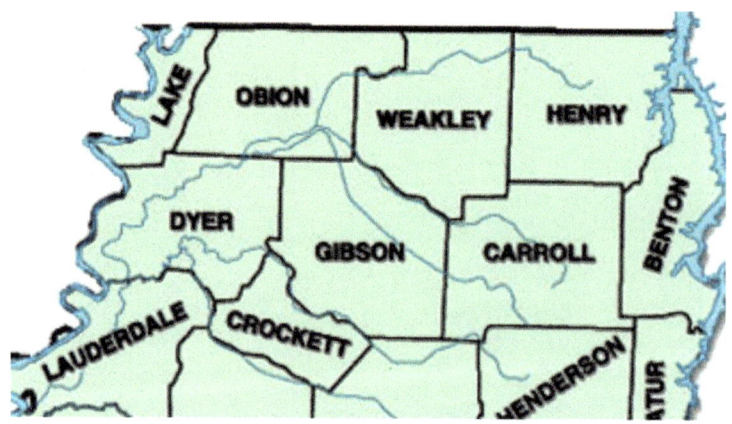

Map of the upper portion of West Tennessee,
used with permission of Charles A. Reeves, Jr.

Lauderdale County, Tennessee, is where author Alex Haley's ancestors settled after the Civil War because the land was so prime and rich that "you plant a pig's tail and a hog'll grow."[19] Life must not have been as prime as expected for Will and Rachel, however, for they were back in Carroll County when their second child, Kathleen Mae Cook, was born on June 15, 1909.

Will's older brother John had moved to Lake County, Tennessee, in 1888 at the age of sixteen. The 1900 census shows him as a tenant farmer living with his wife in District 1 of Lake County.

John bought his first piece of property in 1913, and eventually owned 630 acres in northern Lake County.[20]

The area of Lake County chosen by John Cook was north of the village of Cronanville and between the communities of Bessie and Cates Landing. Cronanville had a general store, cotton gin, grist mill, blacksmith shop, saloon, and Confederate cemetery.[21] The first church in Cronanville was a Cumberland Presbyterian Church in the old Masonic hall at the northwest corner of Cronanville cemetery.[22] Today only the cemetery and a church mark the location of Cronanville.

Preachers at that time often had to be as tough as Dubble-Bubble®. In the 1880's, a preacher was conducting a meeting in an abandoned blacksmith shop near Reelfoot Lake. Preaching in those days was not a soothing message designed to please the ears of the unchurched, but a clear, unvarnished message of warning to the lost. After service one night, a man came for the preacher with a cant-hook. "I'm going to kill that preacher," he said. "If what he preached tonight is true, then I am lost." Fortunately, violence was averted, and the man eventually became a Christian.[23]

People who had little exposure to religion still often knew chimney corner scriptures like "The Lord helps those who help themselves," "An idle mind is the devil's workshop," "Cleanliness is next to Godliness," "Charity begins at home," and "The Lord moves in mysterious ways." A survey of homes in nearby Weakley County in 1883 found that seventy percent of the 2500 families in the county had a Bible in the home.[24] People were often religious in the same way they were Americans – it was something that was part of their basic identity.

Even people who rarely darkened the door of a church building tried to live right and to help each other most of the time. Thomas Jefferson's metaphor of a wall of separation between church and state was slightly off. It was actually a floor of separation because the Judeo-Christian principles of loving God and loving your neighbor were the foundation upon which American civilization rested.

Blacksmith shop of George & John Hopson in Cronanville, photo courtesy of George and Julie Haynes

A photograph of the Cronanville blacksmith shop in the early 1900's appears to show Will Cook standing in a group of men, holding a rubber tire. Rubber bicycle tires were first invented in the 1880's and rubber car tires in the 1890's. The first automobile registrations for Lake County were made in 1906.[25] The first automobile mentioned in northern Lake County was a Brush[26] (made in Detroit from 1907-1913). Over twenty years later, a car tire would be the central object in a tragedy in Will's life.

Will in Carroll Co.   **Man on right -Will?**   **John & Will?**

That Job He's Got to Do

Lake County was one of the last settled places in Tennessee because it was so hard to reach and so inhospitable. The lake and the "scatters" of the lake (the numerous swampy overflows) made travel into the county difficult. David Crockett described wading through a mile and a half of flooded river bottom using poles and trees to bridge the deep spots.[27] Another time, he waded across the mile wide Obion River during winter flooding and nearly froze to death.[28]

Economic opportunities abounded once someone arrived in Lake County. Goodspeed's history said, "the fertility of soil probably surpasses every other county in the state. The soil is a black loam, in many places reaching a depth of ten feet and resting upon a subsoil of sand. ... Originally the county was covered with a heavy growth of poplar, oak, cypress, walnut, beech, and other trees."[29]

At the turn of the twentieth century, the Reelfoot Lake region and Great Lakes region were the most densely wooded forests in the country. Old growth timber was just waiting to be cut. For many years a cottonwood tree stood in Kentucky Bend that measured over thirty feet in circumference.[30]

**Mr. Wilson & Mr. Miller at giant cottonwood tree,
photo courtesy of Winston Whitson**

Chapter Three

Clearing timber from the land was actually three difficult jobs in one: cutting down the tree, cutting it up, and removing the stump. Cutting down a tree gave a man "determination and will power. That's a good thing for a man to have. It goes a long way in his life."[31] Cutting up a tree was usually done with crosscut saws and axes, often in the winter when there were no other farm chores pressing. Sometimes stumps were burned and then chopped and grubbed out of the ground, but the fastest way of removing stumps required three men, a team of mules, and a stump puller. In a day's time, ten to fifteen stumps could be removed this way.[32]

Using a crosscut saw

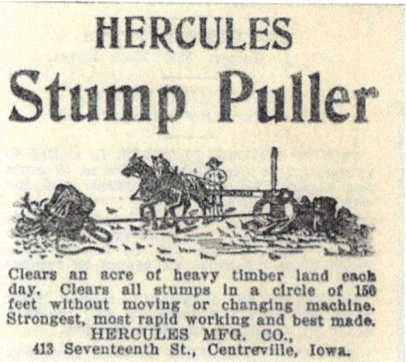

HERCULES

Stump Puller

Clears an acre of heavy timber land each day. Clears all stumps in a circle of 150 feet without moving or changing machine. Strongest, most rapid working and best made.
HERCULES MFG. CO.,
413 Seventeenth St., Centreville, Iowa.

Logging in Obion County

That Job He's Got to Do

Once the timber had been cleared, the land was flat and rich and perfect for raising cotton. A popular saying was that Lake County had "no rocks, no rills, and no hills." In other words, there were no stones, no streams, and nothing but flat land.[33] Besides cotton, other cash crops included corn, hogs, beef cattle, tallow, beef hides, wood for steamboats, and shingles. Fur animals included raccoon, wildcat, wolf, and panther. Hunting and fishing supplemented almost everyone's diet.

A 1908 newspaper advertised 160 acres of Mississippi river bottom land in Lake County near Hickman, Kentucky. It was "Well fenced, five room dwelling house, barn, outhouses, well, etc. 40 acres in cultivation. 40 acres four-years old deadened. Raises from 80 to 100 bushels of corn and from 1500 to 1800 pounds cotton. At least $2000 worth of timber on place." The land was offered for sixteen dollars per acre.[34] This sounds very similar to, and perhaps is the same piece of property purchased by John Cook in 1913.

The year 1910 saw many people predicting the end of the world on May 18 and 19 as Earth passed through the tail of Halley's Comet. Lo and behold, the Earth somehow managed to survive. The lives of Will Cook and family may not have been disrupted by the comet, but big changes were coming in their lives.

Richardsons and Cooks in Carroll County

Chapter Three

The 1910 census shows Will, Rachel, Pauline and Kathleen Cook living in a household in Carroll County. The household of Will's father Dee included Will's niece Ludie, Ludie's husband "Big Cap" Richardson, and their children, Lillian and Dortha. A hired man, Abe Spellings, was also in Dee's household. A picture from about this time shows both Cook households along with Ludie's mother Nancy, probably taken just before all of them (except Dee and Abe) left for Lake County.

Travel to Lake County was difficult, so Big Cap put Ludie, Lillian and Dortha on the train in Humboldt. From there, the train went to Union City, Tennessee, and then to Hickman, Kentucky. From Hickman they took a steamboat to Cates Landing in northern Lake County and then a wagon to their thirty-five acre farm in Bessie. Big Cap, meanwhile, set out on the back of a mule to make the three-day, seventy-mile trip from Carroll County to Lake County.[35]

Mississippi River Landing, Memphis, Tennessee

The Mississippi River played an important part in the lives of Lake Countians. It was both a barrier and a window on the world. The river blocked easy travel to the north and west, but the riverboats allowed access from far away. Many farmers depended on boats to send crops to market. Many businesses depended on supplies brought in by boat. Mark Twain described the scene in a river town when a steamboat arrived:

> "a negro drayman, famous for his quick eye and prodigious voice, lifts up the cry, *S-t-e-a-mboat a-comin'* and the scene changes! The town drunkard stirs, the clerks wake up, a furious clatter of drays follows, every house and store pours out a human contribution, and all in a twinkling the dead town is alive and moving. Drays, carts, men, boys, all go hurrying from many quarters to a common center, the wharf. Assembled there, the people fasten their eyes upon the coming boat as upon a wonder they are seeing for the first time. And the boat *is* rather a handsome sight, too. She is long and sharp and trim and pretty; she has two tall, fancy-topped chimneys, with a gilded device of some kind swung between them; a fanciful pilot-house, all glass and "gingerbread," perched on top of the "texas" deck behind them; the paddle boxes are gorgeous with a picture or with gilded rays above the boat's name; the boiler-deck, the hurricane-deck, and the texas deck are fenced and ornamented with clean white railings; there is a flag gallantly flying from the jack-staff; the furnace doors are open and the fires glaring bravely; the upper decks are black with passengers; the captain stands by the big bell, calm, imposing, the envy of all; great volumes of the blackest smoke are rolling and tumbling out of the chimneys – a husbanded grandeur created with a bit of pitch-pine just before arriving at a town; the crew are grouped on the forecastle; the broad stage is run far out over the port bow, and an envied deck-hand stands picturesquely on the end of it with a coil of rope in his hand, a bell rings, the wheels stop; then they turn back, churning the water to foam, and the steamer is at rest. Then such a scramble as there is to get aboard, and to get ashore, and to take in freight and to discharge freight, all at one and the same time; and such a yelling and cursing as the mates facilitate it all with! Ten minutes later the steamer is under way again, with no flag on the jackstaff and no black smoke issuing from the chimneys. After

ten more minutes the town is dead again, and the town drunkard asleep by the skids once more."[36]

The boats sometimes provided employment opportunities for locals. It also gave them an opportunity to make bad puns, like the time three brothers went to the landing to seek employment on a boat. The mate asked them what they could do. The first two brothers said, "Woodcutter." "Sorry," the mate said, "we don't need any more woodcutters." So they left. When the third brother returned home, the first two brothers were shocked to find he had gotten a job as pilot. "What did you tell the mate?" they asked. "Well," the brother explained, "I said they cut the wood, and I pile it."

"THIS IS NINE-MILE POINT."

Actually, a pilot had the most difficult and important job on a Mississippi River steamboat. The highest rank on the boat belonged to the captain, but the pilot was in charge the whole time the boat was moving. He carried in his head an encyclopedic knowledge of every landmark and landing and all the dangerous shoals, reefs, and snags in the river, together with the knowledge of how to read conditions in a constantly changing river.

The river would not only add new sandbars, reefs, and snags constantly, but would sometimes completely change course. From 1891 to 1905, the river followed a channel that took it right by the western edge of present-day Tiptonville. Then in 1905, the river shifted back to its present channel about a half-mile to the west, turning the old channel into a slough.[37] The river would still be changing course if not for the levee system, possibly cutting across Kentucky Bend or making the Reelfoot Lake bed part of a new channel.

In addition to the pilot, another important steamboat job was the leadsman. He sat on the front of the boat and took soundings of the river depth. His lead line was marked off in fathoms and fractions thereof. The leadsman would sing out the soundings so loudly that the pilot and people on the bank could hear. One fathom (six feet) was "mark one." Two fathoms was "mark twain." All the various fractions of fathoms had names. For example, two and a quarter fathoms (thirteen and a half feet) was "quarter twain." Beyond twenty-five feet, the leadsman would sing out "no bottom!"

Quarter twain! Quarter twain! Mark twain!
by Thomas Hart Benton, with permission of MBI, Inc.

Chapter Three

The boats sometimes provided entertainment for those who had some spending money. Circuses, minstrel shows, magic shows, Shakespeare's plays, comedy shows, singing, dancing, and gambling were all available at one time or another, depending on which boat was at the landing. One resident remembered watching *Romeo and Juliet* on a boat at Cates Landing.[38] One unfortunate boat became stuck on a sandbar outside of Tiptonville. The enterprising crew brought their show into town and performed while waiting for the water to rise.

Kentucky Bend (sometimes called Madrid Bend or Bessie Bend) provided an opportunity for some partying Lake Countians. One could get on board a boat at the bottom of the bend, dance and drink for a few hours while the boat sailed the thirteen miles around the bend, and then get back off just a mile across the land from where one had embarked.[39]

Kentucky Bend resident Norman Parks said, "I came to know the different Lee Line boats by name and could identify each by its whistle. The light-flooded boats steaming by in the night were wonders to behold. ...The calliope of the showboat reached the ear miles away. I liked to watch the giant paddle-wheels kicking up wakes behind them and washing the shore with waves."[40]

"Rounding a Bend" on the Mississippi by Currier & Ives

That Job He's Got to Do

The year 1812 had seen the violent earthquakes that formed Reelfoot Lake. One hundred years later, the spring of 1912 saw flooding in Lake County. On the night of April 5, 1912, the Reelfoot levee broke, and a mile of levee fell into the river. The villages of Reelfoot, Hathaway, and Bessie had to be abandoned. Water covered all of Lake County except a four-by-six-mile strip extending from Tiptonville north. Some people retreated to their upper floors and rooftops. Cows and horses were isolated on "mounds and roofs and scaffolds."[41] About 1,400 refugees crowded into Tiptonville. There were shortages of almost everything. A flood edition of the Tiptonville newspaper was printed on wrapping paper. A whooping cough epidemic broke out, resulting in the deaths of two children.[42]

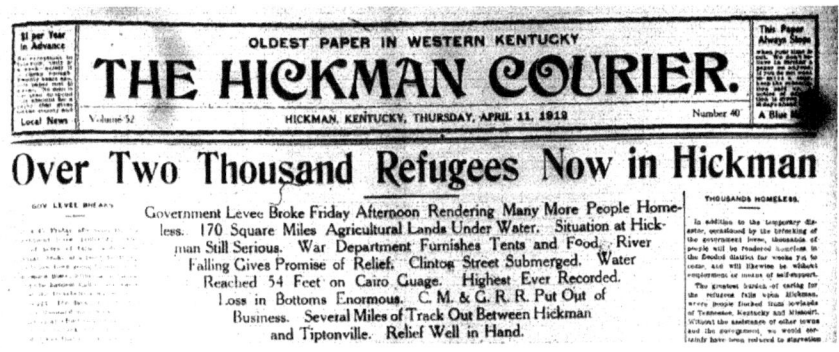

April 1912 Flooding

Chapter Three

Will and Rachel were blessed with twins after their move to Lake County. Woodrow Wilson Cook and Frank Griffin Cook were born August 12, 1912. When the presidential candidate Woodrow Wilson campaigned for office, he promised to make flood control a big part of his administration and also promised to keep America out of the Great War in Europe. These promises no doubt made him a popular figure with Will and Rachel and a worthy namesake for their first-born son. The doctor who delivered them became the namesake for the other twin, Frank Griffin.[43]

Woodrow Wilson

T. F. GRIFFIN, M. D.

The damage from the 1912 floods had not been repaired when more floods came the next year. On January 28, 1913, the Cairo, Illinois, gauge crested at 48.9 feet, and then on April 7, 1913, at 54.7 feet. Back-to-back flood years were unusual and lowered the price of land in the area. In May of 1913, Will's brother John Cook bought 160 acres of land west of the Cates Landing area for eight dollars per acre. In December of the same year after it was revealed that a levee would be built, he bought another 160 acres a little farther north and west along the river for $17.50 per acre.

That Job He's Got to Do

The land John Cook owned was across from Island 10 in the Mississippi River. This was the area where the river had run backwards a hundred years earlier. Just forty years earlier, Island 10 had been the scene of a Civil War naval battle. By the 1900's, however, the relentless current of the river had eaten into the island and into the Tennessee shore and left the remnants of Island 10 against the Missouri shore, separated from it only by a narrow chute.

View from above the land once owned by John Cook, looking northeast at present day Cates Landing

A ground level view across the former Cook lands looking toward a ship at Cates Landing

Chapter Three

The Cates Landing area was home to General Clifton B. Cates, a Marine Corps legend who served in World War I and II. Among other decorations, Cates won a Navy Cross, a Silver Star, and a French Legion of Honor. He rose through the ranks and was one of the few men ever to lead a platoon, a company, a battalion, a regiment, and a division each into combat. Eventually he became Commandant of the Marine Corps. Only a half-mile from the Cates home place, another Marine was born on December 21, 1913, when Will and Rachel's fifth child, William Malcolm Cook, came into the world.

Will Cook's first house in Lake County, possibly John Cook in front.

Lake County's isolation allowed it to retain its unique identity while civilization grew up around it. One writer said, "this region was one of the wildest and most primitive spots perhaps, east of the Rocky Mountains. ... Some students insist that a distinct strain of Chaucerian English is still found here."[44] Another writer said that "much of the spirit of the frontier prevails, and many of the descendants of the earliest settlers have Chickasaw and Cherokee blood in their veins. This folk, while akin to the East Tennessee mountaineers, still retain a western, roving spirit."[45]

A hundred miles to the east, there was a secluded area of the Land Between the Rivers, where the farmers were described as "mountaineers without mountains" because of their close-knit, isolated community.[46] Lake County's isolation, with its mix of pioneering farmers and rugged sportsmen, was more like the rough-and-tumble western frontier. Much of the population was described as yeoman farmers who "disliked city slickers, merchants, banks, Yankees, or anybody who might interfere with their freedom to live as they pleased."[47]

Fishermen's cabin

At the turn of the twentieth century, the Lake County–Reelfoot-Samburg area, while it had many civilized citizens, fine homes, and cultural refinements, might have been described as "frontier surrounded by civilization." It certainly was Tennessee's last frontier. The frontier and civilization, however, were on a collision course that would end with a rise of vigilantes.

Donald V. Sabin photo of duck hunters

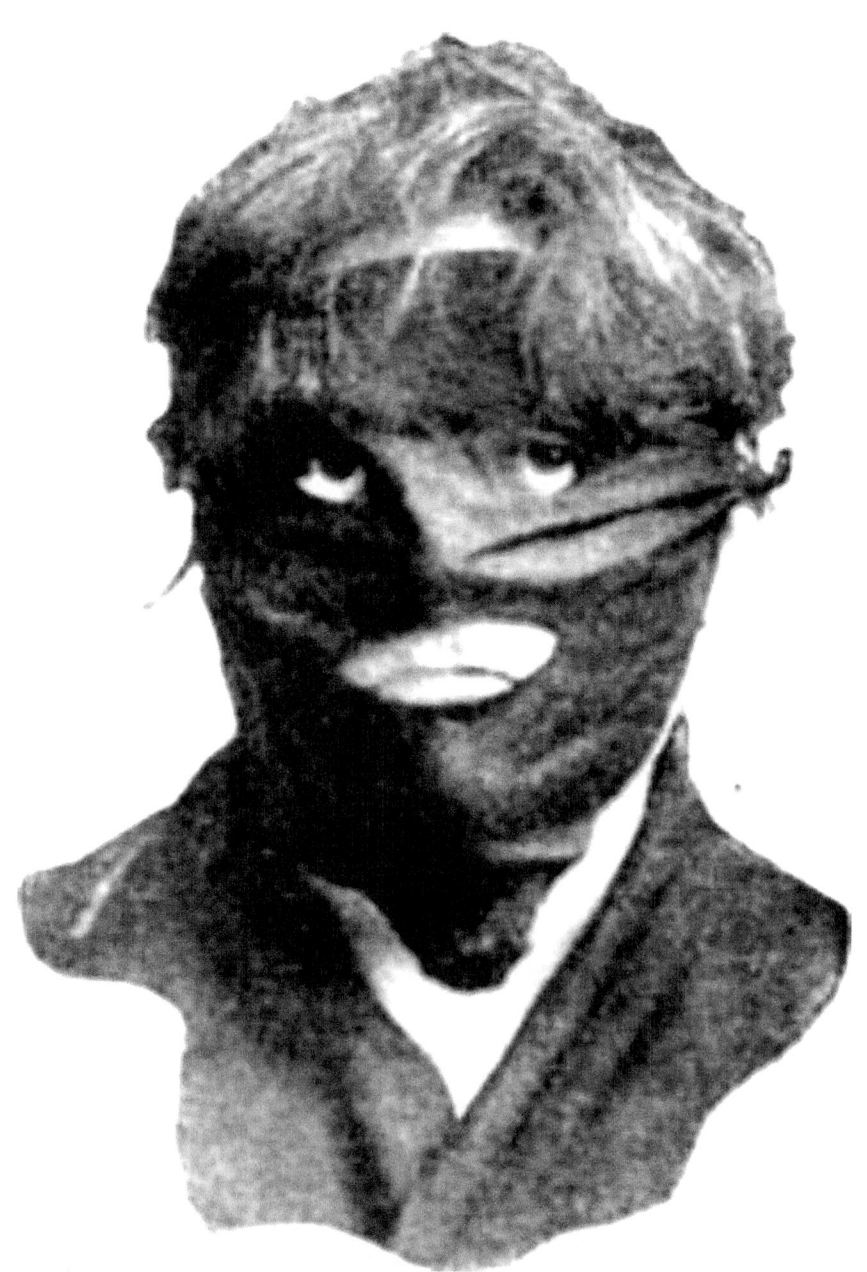

A Night Rider

4.
The Vigilantes

Oh, wonderful lake! You've caused a world of trouble.
            -Annie Somers Gilchrist, *The Night Rider's Daughter*

Reelfoot Lake was born in nature's violence. Almost one hundred years after its birth, it would inspire a period of man-made violence, pitting neighbor against neighbor. This was the time of the Reelfoot Lake Night Riders.

Because of the history of the Ku Klux Klan, the state of Tennessee had passed laws making it illegal for any group to ride at night in disguise.[1] At first, that was the only thing that the Reelfoot Lake Night Riders had in common with the KKK.

The vexing question of the day was, "Who owned Reelfoot Lake?" Before the lake formed, North Carolina had issued land grants for the area. When this land flooded, the grant holders believed they still owned the land beneath the lake. When Tennessee became a state, it issued its own land grants, which often conflicted with North Carolina and federal grants. When David Crockett was in the Tennessee legislature, he promoted the Tennessee Vacant Land bill to help squatters to buy their land, but by the time the legislature finished with the law, it mainly helped the friends of legislators (*plus ça change*). Land grants in Tennessee were a confusing jumble of laws that no one understood.

Possession being nine points of the law, the families who had lived on and worked the land for scores of years believed they had the strongest claim to the land. Tennessee had preemptive grants and occupancy grants to give settlers greater claim to lands they occupied, and some Reelfoot Lake residents may have believed they owned their land. Other residents simply believed that things would remain as they always had, "never once imagining that a spectacled clerk at Nashville would scribble a deed and make some city slicker the owner."[2]

**Young woman holds her baby, Reelfoot Lake,
photo by Albert F. Ganier**

The idea of draining Reelfoot Lake had occurred as early as 1875, when Mr. O.H.P. Bennett of Columbia, Tennessee, proposed the idea. The idea was abandoned at that time because it was believed the bottom of the lake was lower than the bottom of the Mississippi River.[3]

Timber was one inducement for draining the lake. In 1906 a walnut tree was dredged up out of the lake which produced a log three feet in diameter and seventy feet long. "It is free from sap and has no signs of decay and is as black and satiny as the most polished and prepared wood." The log sold for the large sum of one hundred dollars.[4]

In 1899, James Harris announced that he had bought all the land around and under the lake. He said he would drain part of the lake, harvest the timber, and turn 15,000 acres into farmland. He brought in 175 teams of mules to begin clearing a path for a drainage canal beginning at the washout area.[5] Harris certainly believed he was improving the local area. As he said, "Are the lakes and swamps to remain, producing malaria, snakes, buffalo gnats, and mosquitoes, or be drained off and utilized for the public good?"[6]

No matter how thin you slice the baloney, it's still got two sides.[7] Some people supported the idea of draining part of the swamp land and turning it into productive farm land. Others were horrified at the idea. Many residents joined together in legal action to try to stop the draining of the lake. When James Harris died in 1903, his son, Judge Harris, at first continued his plan to drain the lake but then changed to the idea of making Reelfoot a private lake.

Some have characterized the period of the Night Riders as a conflict between the civilized "southern gentry" in Tiptonville and the frontier "ruffians" who lived on the eastern side of the lake near Samburg.[8] The most active of the Night Riders did live on the eastern side of the lake, but there were people on both sides of the issue all around the lake. Legal action to preserve the lake continued.

Lake supporters were successful at first in saving the lake. Then some of their lawyers saw an opportunity to profit by their knowledge. They changed sides and formed the West Tennessee Land Company which allied with Mr. Harris to control the lake.[9] Lake supporters felt betrayed and outraged.

Many of these lake supporters saw vigilante action as their only recourse. Across the border in Kentucky a few years earlier, a group of vigilantes had organized in support of a tobacco growers' union. (This was the subject of Robert Penn Warren's first novel, *Night Rider*.) Their methods of organization were copied by the Reelfoot Lake Night Riders.

The Kentucky Night Riders had been union enforcers. The Reelfoot Lake Night Riders were environmental activists, perhaps the first in American history. These preservationists may have been primarily interested in preserving their own incomes, but their battle foreshadowed many conflicts that would take place in America between those wanting to preserve the land and those wanting to develop it for the greatest good for the greatest number of people.

There were at least a hundred families around the lake who made the bulk of their livelihood, or at least supplemented it, by hunting and fishing.[10] The Night Riders probably had about two hundred members. Many farm hands and laborers joined. Some joined simply for the adventure.[11] Some hid their activities by going "hunting" at night. Perhaps only twenty of the members were very active. A large percentage of the population, however, sympathized with the Night Riders.[12]

In later years, Will Cook told his son that he had been a member of the Night Riders,[13] but he could not have been very active. In 1908, when the Night Riders were operating, he was living in Carroll and Lauderdale County, but his brother John lived in Lake County. It was during this time that Will was searching for greater economic opportunities, so he easily could have visited his brother and participated in some Night Rider activities. Possibly John was a member also.

At first, the Night Riders focused on the lake. They burnt the fishing docks of J.C. Burdick (who was caught in the middle between the fishermen and the Land Company). They had frequent meetings to talk about their goals. They typically met on the east side of the lake at Bogus Hollow or at the Fitz Smith sawdust pile or in Buck Eskew woods. "Among the speakers appeared notables from the region, men who encouraged the movement, but who could not ride with it for professional reasons. The riders counted on these educated sympathizers to acquaint outsiders with their complaints and to lead the search for a solution."[14] Some say the riders also did benevolent acts that helped poor people around the lake.[15]

The problem with vigilante groups is the lack of control, and the Night Riders were no exception. They had trouble staying focused on their main objective. The riders had several gangs who sometimes operated independently.[16] They sometimes acted like a chicken with his head cut off, terrorizing people who had nothing to do with controlling the lake. They whipped people they believed weren't living right. They whipped a man who insulted them, and he later died of his injuries. They became so drunk on their power that one night they took over the town of Hornbeak and forced a band to play tunes for them. Every other song had to be "Dixie."

Riders with no moral compass were often able to provoke hotheads in the group to take extreme action. Bootlegger Frank Feheringer from Hickman, Kentucky, was a petty criminal who became a leader in the group. He helped lead the Riders on their two worst crimes.[17]

On October 3, 1908, about fifty Riders traveled across the state line to Brownsville, Kentucky, looking for a man named Dave Walker. Some reports say Walker was an "insolent negro."[18] Some reports said that he had insulted a white woman and pulled a gun on a white man.[19] One report said that they were looking for Walker and two other men who had raped a white woman.[20] Another report said that the Kentucky sheriff had asked the Riders to come and "take care" of Walker.[21]

When Walker refused to come out, the Riders set fire to his house. One of the Riders was killed by shots fired from the house. As the fire consumed the house, the Riders killed Walker, his twelve year old daughter, and his wife and baby as they fled.[22] Three children were only injured; they may have survived by "playing possum." News of the massacre brought cries of outrage from across the country. The governor of Kentucky expressed outrage and offered a five-hundred-dollar reward for the apprehension of the perpetrators.

The local paper in Hickman, Kentucky, was not so full of outrage. An editorial said that Walker was "no saint."[23] No one was ever arrested for the crime.

Eighteen days after the Walker massacre, the Reelfoot Lake Night Riders took their last ride. Robert Taylor and Captain Quentin Rankin were the lawyers from Trenton, Tennessee, who earlier had worked for the lake supporters. Then these lawyers had used knowledge that they gained while working for the lake supporters to switch sides, form the West Tennessee Land Company, and enrich themselves. If their actions weren't illegal, they were certainly unethical. Rankin would pay with his life.

On October 21, 1908, Taylor and Rankin made the unfortunate decision to visit Reelfoot Lake to work out some leases. The Riders found out, and about thirty-five of them forced Taylor and Rankin from their hotel in the Walnut Log area of Reelfoot. They put a rope around Rankin's neck and raised and lowered him while demanding he rescind the privatization of the lake. He refused, further enraging the crowd.

Hickman Courier, October 22, 1908

That Job He's Got to Do

According to local writer Walter Edgar Lowe, "There is a tradition around the lake that the Night Riders had no intention of killing Captain Rankin, but merely intended to frighten the two men ... It has been said that some of them acting under the impulse of whiskey decided on the spur of the moment to kill Rankin."[24] Shots were fired, and Quentin Rankin was dead. Fellow lawyer Robert Taylor dived into a slough and escaped in spite of many shots fired in his direction.

Nashville Banner, October 21, 1908

The national outrage was overwhelming. Governor Patterson of Tennessee called out the militia, which arrested hundreds of suspects. Thirty-two men were tried. One of the riders died from congestive chills and another from malaria while awaiting trial. Six men were convicted. All convictions were overturned on procedural rules. Two of the men were retried but released after a hung jury. No one else was retried.

Lake County News, December 31, 1908

Chapter Four

Night Riders going to court: L-R, 1 Tid Burton, 3 Garrett Johnson, 5 Sam Applewhite, 6 Fred Pinion, 8 Arthur Cloar, 9 Roy Ransom.

The Tennessee Supreme Court ruled in April 1913 that Reelfoot Lake was navigable and therefore public property. The West Tennessee Land Company's title to the lake was made void, and it received $25,000 for its claims. J.C. Burdick received $2000 for his fishing lease. Judge Harris, the man behind the controversy, drowned in 1913 while swimming in the lake he had once owned.

The purchase of the lake by the state ensured that the lake would remain open to everyone. It also led to the creation of the State Department of Game and Fish which regulated hunting and fishing on Reelfoot Lake.[25] The Night Riders had followed a crooked road and committed some terrible crimes, but they believed they had a job to do in saving the lake, and they did it. That is why some people around the lake today consider the Night Riders to be heroes rather than villains.

That Job He's Got to Do

Cotton field between Reelfoot Lake and Tiptonville

5.
King Cotton

Oh, I wish I was in the land of cotton,
Old times there are not forgotten.

-Daniel Decatur Emmett, *Dixie*

It is doubtful whether there has ever been a plant so connected to the history of a country as cotton has been to the United States. Cotton was America's most important export from 1803 to 1937. The United States silver dollar minted in the late 1800's featured a Lady Liberty wearing a crown made of cotton and wheat, symbolizing the importance of those crops.  Cotton even played an important role in the Battle of New Orleans; the Seventh Infantry Regiment of the United States Army is still known today as the Cottonbalers.

Millions of people depended on cotton for their livelihood. Millions of Africans and their descendants were enslaved because of cotton. The war between cotton-growing and cotton-consuming states claimed the lives of six hundred thousand men.

The first cotton gin in West Tennessee was built in Jackson in 1821. Lake County, the last frontier of Tennessee, did not get its first gin (a horse-powered gin at Pea Ridge) until 1865. Cotton requires a growing season of two hundred frost-free days. A period of climate change began a warming trend about 1890, and cotton became easier to grow in Lake County. By 1900, there were gins in Kentucky Bend, Bessie, Cates, Cronanville, and Tiptonville.[1]

Cotton tended to encourage large landowners. In the 1920's, Lake County had a total of 140 property owners, but fifteen individuals owned most of the land, and tenants did most of the work.[2] Across the South, sixty percent of the people whose lives depended on cotton owned no houses or land. These were tenant farmers, who struggled constantly on the edge of financial ruin, starvation, and disease.[3]

A typical poor farm family

There were several types of tenant farmers, and the systems varied from place to place. Generally the landowner would furnish a house, firewood, well, and a plot of land for growing vegetables and keeping animals. The highest form of tenant farming was called "standing rent." These tenants had their own farm stock and equipment and could obtain credit to furnish their own provisions. They paid the landowner a fixed or standing rent for each acre of property that they cultivated and got to keep everything they produced. The tenants at the next level were on "thirds and fourths." They furnished their provisions, their seed, and part of their fertilizer and paid the landowner a third of their cotton and a fourth of their corn. The next level of tenant was the sharecropper who was "on halves." He furnished only his provisions and paid the landowner half the crop. Some tenants had considerably worse deals, perhaps paying out three-fourths of the crop. Finally, there were wage laborers, or "hired men." They received a monthly wage and "found," that is, food. Typical "found" for a week was three-and-a-half pounds of bacon, a peck (one-fourth bushel) of meal, a half-gallon of syrup, and a plug of tobacco. Like all tenants, hired men grew their own vegetables and hunted their own game.[4]

Will Cook was a tenant farmer. Since his landowner was his brother John, we presume that he had a better deal than the average tenant. Perhaps Will also served as an overseer of the other tenants. Whatever his financial compensation, Will nevertheless had a grueling existence. Tenant farmers worked from sunup to sundown, and there was always a job that needed to be done.

The tenant farmer and his wife would rise about four o'clock in the morning. She would begin breakfast while he went out and rang the dinner bell. This was the signal for the hands to rise, eat a bite, harness their teams, and prepare to hook up to the equipment for the day's work. "There was much singing, joking, and tale-telling during the hooking-up and waiting period... They all enjoyed a sense of humor and genuine love and concern for each other."[5] "The men took a lantern to the gear room, harnessed the mules, and before daybreak, they would be waiting with the plow, planter, or cultivator ... until it got light enough to see down the row."[6] When the sun came up, all hands would be in the field at work.

After guiding the mule all morning, the farmer would stop when the dinner bell rang at 11:30. He would take the mules to the barn to rest and get fresh water. Then he would go to his house to eat dinner. Dinner might be some combination of fried chicken, bacon, bologna, crackers, fat-back, sausage, biscuits, white beans, cornbread, canned fruit, and cake.[7] After dinner there would be a short period of rest until 12:30 or 1:00, when the bell would ring to begin the afternoon work.[8]

The dinner bell was necessary because a pocket watch would not withstand the rigors of farm work. They were only carried to town or to church. Wrist-watches were even more fragile, and no man at the time would wear one lest he be considered lady-like.[9]

The rich, alluvial soil of Lake County was kind to farmers. An *acre* had originally measured the amount of land a man could plow in a day. Hard-working Lake County farmers could do much better than that, plowing perhaps as much as eight acres in a day.[10]

One farmer was known for singing to his mules as he plowed. The mules would keep cadence with the singing. He had to keep two teams of mules, one for the morning and one for the afternoon, because one team could not hold up all day at his pace.[11]

**A team of mules pulling a harrow,
courtesy of the Emmett Lewis Museum in Tiptonville.**

That Job He's Got to Do

The church song "Work for the Night is Coming"[12] would reso-
nate with farmers like Will. Its admonition to "work till the last
beam fadeth" and "work while the night is darkening" may have
been figurative phrases about life, but they applied literally to the
farmer. When the evening sun touched the horizon (and it is a
very low horizon in Lake County), Will would head for the barn,
care for the stock, and finish other chores until it was time to go
to the house for supper. Tenant farmers would typically go to bed
with the chickens.

Planting cottonseed in New Madrid County, Missouri.

The yearly schedule for cotton began in February with breaking
the ground, turning it, and bedding it to prepare for planting.
Then fertilizing must be done, then planting, and then "sweep-
ing" or cultivating out the weeds. As soon as the plants were tall
enough, the whole family participated in chopping the cotton.
This was the process of thinning the plants down to a few stalks
per hill. Hills were spaced every twelve to sixteen inches apart.
Chopping a field of cotton would cause your body to ache from
your arms all the way down to the end of your spine.[13] The whole
family also participated in hoeing weeds until July, when the

cotton was "laid by." That is, nothing else would be done to the fields until time to pick.

Besides working the cotton fields, there were also fields of corn and alfalfa to plant and fields of hay to cut. In the fall there was corn to harvest and shell. Late fall was hog-killing time. There was always stock to feed and take care of, such as checking the animals for sores where the equipment fit or taking a mule to be shod or milking the cow. In the winter after everything was harvested, it was time to sharpen saws and axes, chop down trees, and cut wood until plowing time came around again.

A farmer with his mule.

"Use it up, wear it out, make it do, or do without" were essential rules for the farmer. "Life is too short to waste a day being unhappy. If something is broke, fix it. If something is missing, find it. Learn to live with and love what you have."[14] Not one iota was thrown away. Food scraps were given to the animals. Broken tools were fixed or used as parts for other things. There would always be broken wagon wheels to fix or plow points to sharpen or harnesses to repair. A tenant farmer was as busy as a cranberry merchant at Christmastime; there was always a job he had to do.

The first bolls of cotton began opening in August. Picking began soon after and continued through the end of the year. Schools would start in August and then turn out at the end of September so students could spend some time in the fields.[15]

That Job He's Got to Do

Picking cotton required one to walk bent over while dragging a heavy nine-foot sack or a large basket. People with bad backs would sometimes crawl along the rows. The fingers soon became sore and bleeding from the sharp tips of the cotton burrs. John Grisham described the picking experience as, "tearing the fluffy bolls from the stalks at a steady pace, stuffing them into the heavy sack, afraid to look down the row and be reminded of how endless it was, afraid to slow down because someone would notice. My fingers would bleed, my neck would burn, my back would hurt."[16]

Picking cotton in Oklahoma.

The amount of cotton a person could pick in a day varied considerably. A child might pick 25 pounds, using a tow sack (burlap bag) or a flour sack. An average adult might pick 300 pounds. An adult who wouldn't hit a lick at a snake might pick 125 pounds.

Someone who was walking in high cotton might occasionally pick 500 pounds in a day. Pickers called this "picking a bale of cotton" in a day, and some in Will's family did this.[17] A bale of *ginned* cotton weighs 500 pounds, so this is where the expression originated, but to actually pick a bale of cotton in a day would require picking 1500 pounds of *raw* cotton, or over 150,000 cotton bolls, which is impossible for a human picker.[18]

Chapter Five

Weighing cotton, courtesy Emmett Lewis Museum in Tiptonville.

The farm wagon would be fitted with side boards and parked in the middle of the field. A set of scales would be hung on the brake pole, and periodically, a picker would take his sack to the wagon, where it would be weighed and emptied. When the wagon had 1500 pounds of raw cotton, it was ready to go to the gin. The gin would remove the seeds and trash and compress the cotton into about a 500-pound bale.

A general store was often close to the cotton gin. The general mercantile stores in farm towns were the supercenters of their day. They stocked barrels of flour, sugar, and molasses. They had rope, harness, horse collars, singletrees, trace chains, bridles, saddles, horseshoes, cotton-picking sacks, paint, hoes, rakes, shovels, pitchforks, kerosene, firearms, knives, shirts, shoes, hats, overalls, dress material, lace, needles, thread, bandannas, jewelry, coffee beans, crackers in a barrel, cheese in a hoop, souse, pickled pigs' feet, tobacco, canned goods, bacon, fruit, dried beans, and penny candy.[19]

Once a family had taken all of their cotton to the gin and been paid, they would settle up their old accounts at the store. Then, they might leave for home with a barrel of sugar, a barrel of molasses, four or five barrels of flour, a box or two of bacon, some meal, some coffee, and a few pieces of clothing for the family.[20] This would have to last them until the next harvest, supplemented only by what the store would extend them on credit.

In a good year the farmer might get some extra spending money, but cotton prices, like the weather, were unpredictable. In 1912, cotton sold on the Memphis market for twelve cents per pound. By 1919, war demands had almost tripled the price to thirty-five cents per pound. The next year, it dropped back to fifteen cents per pound.

The price of cotton and the amount of cotton produced were often affected by natural disasters and insects.[21] The boll weevil blight, which began in the West, began spreading east of the Mississippi after 1915. Floods, as we've seen, occurred in 1912 and 1913. The Cook family enjoyed good farming for three straight years after those floods, but then disaster struck again.

The year 1917 began disagreeably, with the weather so cold that the river froze.[22] Halfway around the world in Russia, a revolution began in March that would create misery throughout the twentieth century and beyond. In April, America entered the Great War being fought in Europe. Will Cook, who was forty-two years old with six children, was not called to serve.

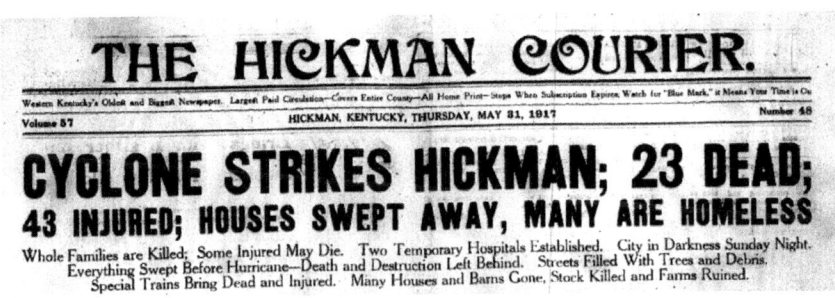

THE HICKMAN COURIER.

Western Kentucky's Oldest and Biggest Newspaper. Largest Paid Circulation—Covers Entire County—All Home Print—Stops When Subscription Expires. Watch for "Blue Mark," it Means Your Time is Out

Volume 57　　　　　HICKMAN, KENTUCKY, THURSDAY, MAY 31, 1917　　　　　Number 48

CYCLONE STRIKES HICKMAN; 23 DEAD;
43 INJURED; HOUSES SWEPT AWAY, MANY ARE HOMELESS

Whole Families are Killed; Some Injured May Die. Two Temporary Hospitals Established. City in Darkness Sunday Night. Everything Swept Before Hurricane—Death and Destruction Left Behind. Streets Filled With Trees and Debris. Special Trains Bring Dead and Injured. Many Houses and Barns Gone, Stock Killed and Farms Ruined.

In May of 1917, a tornado outbreak began that was one of the most intense and longest in recorded history. It lasted eight days, spawned seventy-three tornadoes, and took 383 lives.[23] One of those tornadoes occurred on Sunday, May 27 at four o'clock in the afternoon. It was an F4 tornado that swept across northern Lake County, Tennessee, and into Kentucky.

Chapter Five

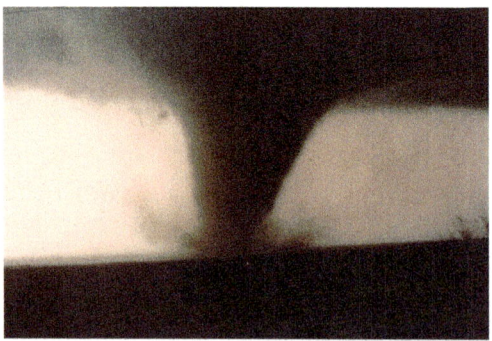

A typical F4 tornado

Will Cook opened his front door that afternoon and said, "Something's coming!" By the time he got the door closed, the house was beginning to blow away. Two of his daughters, Pauline and Kathleen, ages nine and seven, were outside and tried to go into the barn. They couldn't get in because the door was stuck, but they survived as the storm passed.[24]

This tornado killed sixty-five people in Kentucky and two in Tennessee. One of the two people killed in Tennessee was Georgia Lyons, a thirty-year-old black woman who was just outside the Cook residence. Pauline, Kathleen, and Griffin watched as the lady was rolled up in fence wire and carried away by the tornado.

Four-year-old Griffin was blown for perhaps two miles by the tornado but survived. When he was found, he was so far from home and so bloody that for a time his rescuers didn't know who he was.[25] All he could tell them was that his name was "Diffin Took." He lived at the doctor's house for several weeks and fully recovered, but he bore a large scar on his forehead for the rest of his life.

Griffin, at age 84, with youngest grandchild and scar on forehead

Will, his wife, and four of their children were injured by the tornado. Will and Rachel's sixth child L.D. (named for Will's father Lawrence Decatur) had been born October 9, 1916. Rachel, holding L.D., was injured and bore scars on her arms and legs for a long time. Neighbors J.M. Alexander, George Alexander, Mattie Lee, Mr. and Mrs. Ben LeDuke, and Mrs. Will Bass and her four children were also injured. Four houses were blown into the river.[26] The Hickman, Kentucky newspaper of May 31, 1917, incorrectly reported that John Cook and his son had been killed by the tornado.

Tornado damage in the Cronanville area, Emma Wigdor photo.

It's been said that lightning doesn't strike twice in the same place. This area hit by a tornado, however, had been hit by another tornado fifty-five years earlier. On April 2, 1862, during the battle of Island 10 in the Civil War, a tornado followed this same track through northern Lake County. It killed six soldiers, injured many, and damaged some of the Union boats involved in the battle.[27]

In addition to the half-mile-wide path of destruction through Bessie, Cronanville, Cates Landing, and Phillippy, the 1917 tornado also had some freakish results. A straw was driven into a tree, and a large mule was lodged in the fork of a tree twenty feet off the ground.[28] The other person killed in Tennessee by this tornado was Sam Littleton, a twenty-four-year-old black man who was blown a half-mile across a field.[29] His death certificate says he "met instant death in the cyclone." The same day, a different tornado toward the southeast killed seven people in Dyer County and five people in Weakley County.

After the tornado there were lots of jobs to do in rebuilding what was destroyed. Fortunately, Will's brother John was somewhat prosperous and could afford to rebuild the homes on his property. John Cook owned a store, which allowed him not only to make money on the cotton he raised but also on the supplies he sold to others.[30] John was a successful farmer and businessman but suffered some tragedies in his personal life.

Home of John Cook

John Cook had moved on his own from Carroll County to Lake County in 1888 at the age of sixteen. At age twenty-four, he married a Carroll County girl who died six years later, perhaps from smallpox. John then married a woman from Dyer County.[31] They had one child, John Jr., who died in 1919 at the age of twelve from tetanus. The tetanus developed from a contaminated wound in young John's foot, possibly from being stepped on by a mule or from stepping on a rusty nail.

Tetanus was a horrible disease. Antibiotics were created twenty years too late to help young John Cook. One home remedy at the time said, "If you stick a nail in your foot, crush up a raw cucumber and put it on the place to prevent 'proud flesh.'"[32] The only medical treatment available at the time for tetanus was sedatives for pain.

As the tetanus infection progressed, muscle spasms spread through the body. These usually began in the jaw, giving the name lockjaw to the disease. As it spread through the nervous system, powerful and painful muscle contractions occurred in the neck, chest, back, abdomen, and legs. Other symptoms included fever, hypersensitivity, drooling, difficulty swallowing, and loss of control of bladder and bowels. Death, when it came, was often a relief.

After losing their only child, John Cook and his wife needed a break from their lives. Fortunately, they had the financial resources to take a long vacation. The census of 1920 shows them living in a rented house in St. Petersburg, Florida. Later, they returned to Lake County, possibly in April 1921, when John and Will's father Dee passed away at age eighty-five.

King Cotton made John Cook more money than Carter had oats.[33] It made a living possible for Will Cook and his family, but there was a lot of inequality in the cotton economy. A third of the cotton tenants across the South were black. For them the cotton economy was typically less favorable. You could find "negro foremen, negro overseers, negro small farmers, and even negro landlords. Generally speaking though, the negro is a lot worse off, on the land, than the white man." If you want an idea of the condition of the average black tenant, take the condition of the average white tenant, "Then take away the garden. And the hog... And the cow... And reduce the amount of corn, and peas and sorghum."[34]

Life on the Mississippi, by Thomas Hart Benton

6.
Killed a Nigger

"We blowed out a cylinder head."
"Good gracious! Anybody hurt?"
"No'm. Killed a nigger."
"Well, it's lucky, because sometimes people do get hurt."

- Mark Twain, *Adventures of Huckleberry Finn*

Samuel Clemens classic novel about Huck Finn uses the word *nigger* over 200 times. Some people believe, because of this, that the novel is offensive to black people, but surely they have not read it. If we want to understand either Mark Twain or Will Cook, we need to understand the state of race relations in America in their time.

The first black man in America probably arrived with Hernando de Soto's expedition in 1540.[1] Blacks were brought to America in great numbers beginning in 1619, when a Portuguese trading vessel landed twenty African slaves in Jamestown, Virginia.[2] For purposes of this study, however, we may skip ahead 240 years to the beginnings of the Civil War. Slavery, at that point, was beginning to be regarded not as "a peculiar institution," but as a terrible cancer in a nation that had declared "All men are created equal." John Quincy Adams called slavery "the great and foul stain on the North American Union."[3] The "fire bell in the night" that Jefferson had predicted was being heard.[4]

Tragically, there were slave owners who beat, raped, and mistreated their slaves in every way.

> I saw a savage overseer tie a negro slave, Patrick by name, to a log and draw a wild black cat, by the tail, down the negro's naked back, from his shoulders to his heels. The infernal process was thrice repeated. Patrick shrieked and swooned. A strong solution of salt and vinegar was then

poured over the senseless negro's back. When he recovered his senses he was gagged. He wore the gag, constantly moving it to one side, till it carved a slit in the corner of his mouth. The hapless negro could talk a little and drink a little, still wearing the gag. It was made of iron, having hinges, and was locked behind his neck. A flat piece of iron, projecting inwardly, from the rim, entered the mouth. I describe it because, having lived always in the South, it was the only 'gag' I ever saw. When Patrick could talk, eat, or drink, wearing the gag, the overseer belled him. An iron belt about the body and another around the neck sustained an iron rod extending along the spine, three feet above Patrick's head. To the end of this rod a bell was attached; and wearing all this machinery of iron, Patrick was forced by the fiend incarnate to pick cotton. [5]

"Every story is more complicated, and generally more interesting, than it first appears."[6] This is certainly true of the story of slavery and the war. Too often when history is taught, reality leaves the room.[7] Many slave owners had a complex relationship with their slaves. Booker T. Washington, who was born a slave, described an upbringing of terrible hardships and wants, but continued this way:

> "One may get the idea from what I have said that there was bitter feeling toward the white people on the part of my race... this was not true, and it was not true of any large portion of the slave population in the South where the Negro was treated with anything like decency."[8]

Some slave owners felt they had a fatherly relationship with their slaves and were genuinely surprised to find that the slaves wanted freedom. As a South Carolina planter said, "I believed that these people were content, happy, and attached to their masters."[9]

Indeed, many slaves had a strong bond to their owner that made it *seem* they preferred slavery over freedom. When one Confederate soldier was captured at the battle of Island 10, his slave Paris was offered thirty dollars per month to cook for the

Union army. Instead, Paris and seven other blacks escaped, crossed Reelfoot Lake, and completed a two-week rail and riverboat journey back to their home in Alabama.[10]

A very few slave owners freed their slaves in the years before the war. One who did so at great cost to himself was Granville Lipscomb of Franklin County, Tennessee. Studying the Bible had led Granville to realize that "Where the spirit of the Lord is, there is liberty."[11] Since it was not legal to free his slaves in Tennessee, Lipscomb moved his family to Sangamon County, Illinois, in 1835. There he could free his slaves across the border in the Indiana territory. He successfully freed the slaves, but tragically, Granville's wife and three of his children contracted malaria in Illinois and died. Granville moved back to Tennessee with his son, David, who would eventually start a Bible school in Nashville that became David Lipscomb College.[12]

Will Cook's grandfather had owned a slave, but Will's father had fought for the Union. Many people had perspectives on freedom, slavery, and the war that seem bizarre to modern sensibilities. There was a West Tennessee planter who owned forty-six slaves before the war but was a strong unionist and held Republican offices after the war, even though Republicans were the ones who had freed the slaves.[13] Although Robert E. Lee would lead the Southern armies that were trying to preserve slavery, he had written to his wife in 1856 that slavery "is a moral and political evil in any country."[14]

The Civil War was a conflict in which each side believed it had a righteous cause. The Unionists believed that preserving the Union or freeing the slaves were the greatest goals. The Secessionists believed, as Alexander Hamilton had said, that "The origin of all civil government, justly established, must be a voluntary compact."[15] They believed that the right to leave was the greater cause.

Abraham Lincoln is a complicated figure in American history. On one hand, he is to be greatly honored for freeing the slaves. On the other, he is to be condemned for causing six hundred

Chapter Six

thousand men to be killed in the process. It is sad that a government that claimed it didn't have the money or the authority to enforce the laws against importation of slaves or to regulate the interstate commerce in slaves or to buy all the slaves and free them, somehow found both the authority and the money to wage war on its former member states.[16]

If today there were states which were pro-choice on the subject of abortion, for example, New York and California, and those states were invaded by armies from Texas and Utah, and if those armies went about killing, looting, and burning until the states became pro-life, then the people in those states would have an idea of the kind of outrage that many Southerners felt when invaded by Yankees. And the outrage wouldn't end when the armies left; it would remain for many generations.

So, it was a wonderful thing that the slaves were freed, but the war was the worst possible way to do it. A popular war-mongering song at the time spoke euphemistically of "trampling out the vintage where the grapes of wrath are stored." The South felt the brunt of the Union's "terrible swift sword" as everyone in its path was trampled.

> "Soun' like de Yankees ain't leaving nothin'! Dem white mens swears dey's burnin' de fiels, de big houses, de barns! Dey's killin' de mules an' cookin' de cows an everythin' else dey can eat! Whatever dey ain't burnin' an' eatin' dey's jes' ruinin', plus stealin' anythin' dey can tote off!"

- Alex Haley, *Roots*[17]

"A blight descended on the land" from 1860 to 1865."[18] Satan must have been laughing with delight. Union General Charles Smith of the Second Division of the Army of the Tennessee visited the town of McKenzie in Carroll County, Tennessee. Mrs. Annie Cole Hawkins described their actions:

> "I can never forget the sickening scene when they began their work of destruction. Bursting open the doors, tearing down and burning fences and gates, cutting and breaking up the family carriage, killing cattle, hogs, sheep, geese,

turkeys, chickens, and every living thing they could lay their cowardly hands on. ... The ruffians took all they wanted to eat and carry off, then piled the rest with the nice white lard and made a bonfire of it right at our window just for the sake of destroying."[19]

In northern Alabama, Gen. Grenville Dodge of the Union Army XVI Corps lit up the Tennessee valley with the flames of burning houses and stables. Col. Florence Cornyn of the Seventh Illinois destroyed everything from houses to corn-cribs. When Gen. James Wilson of the Union's Military Division of the Mississippi finished his killing spree, the road from Planterville to Selma, Alabama, was covered with dead horses and mules.[20]

Union forces in Huntsville, Alabama, took delight in stabling their horses inside all the local church buildings. In Obion County, Tennessee, Jensen's Seventh Kansas Cavalry stopped a funeral procession and opened the casket to check for contraband. Finding nothing but the body of the deceased, they stole the mules which had been pulling the hearse.[21]

Robert Cartmell, the Jackson, Tennessee, farmer who had declared before the war that "the union ought to be preserved," was visited by Col. Nobles and the Second Illinois Cavalry. Cartmell described the result:

> "House burned down, fencing pretty well all burned, not an acre enclosed on the place, no hogs – about 130 killed. My cattle, except 2 milk cows, killed. 1 mule and 3 good horses taken; found my gin house and lint room injured, all the floors taken. The planks or weather boarding and part of the roof of lint room and most of the boarding of the gin houses gone. My gin stands broken to pieces and ruined, every cast wheel broke, saws bent, part of the fan and thresher taken. My harness run through the cutting knife and cut in pieces about an inch long. My timber going fast. Farming implements destroyed or burnt up. Had most of them packed away in cellar. At least 1000 barrels corn foraged away by the Cavalry encamped."[22]

Chapter Six

The Union did not just defeat but destroyed much of the South. Those who supported secession and those who supported the Union, along with those who were freed from slavery, all had to struggle to survive. As W.E.B. DuBois noted, "gaunt Hunger wept beside Bereavement."[23]

After enduring defeat, the South had to endure Reconstruction. DuBois called Reconstruction a "splendid failure." Most Southerners saw nothing splendid about it. "Malice toward none and charity for all" were forgotten as the U.S. Congress managed to mistreat almost everyone (*plus ça change*). Former slaves never received the forty acres and a mule they were promised. Northern teachers came south to teach former slaves to distrust whites, to segregate themselves from whites as much as possible, and to give up all former habits such as showing respect for white men and women.[24] "The business of educating the negroes was a continuation of hostilities against the vanquished South."[25]

DuBois said of the former slaves, "They fled to the friends that had freed them, even though those friends stood ready to use them as a club for driving the recalcitrant South back into loyalty."[26]

Booker T. Washington wrote:[27]

> "I felt that the Reconstruction policy, so far as it related to my race, was in a large measure on a false foundation, was artificial and forced. In many cases it seemed to me that the ignorance of my race was being used as a tool with which to help white men into office, and that there was an element in the North which wanted to punish the Southern white men by forcing the Negro into positions over the heads of the Southern whites. I felt that the Negro would be the one to suffer for this in the end."

Slaves did not start the Civil War and did not inflict Reconstruction upon the South, but as Booker T. Washington predicted, they and their descendants suffered the bitter harvest of anger, resentment, and division that followed for generations to come. And when Satan sows anger and division, there are far too many who are willing to cultivate that crop.

Tenant farm children

It is a long, steep climb from slavery to equality, which continues to this day. It has been made more difficult, not only by the evil done directly to blacks, but also by self-fulfilling racist attitudes about them. Even people who felt kindly toward blacks often felt their limited capabilities weren't worth much of an investment. Harvard historian Albert Bushnell Hart, the mentor of W.E.B. DuBois, considered the average black man to be a "moral and social cripple."[28] A Baptist leader in Montgomery, Alabama, had this charitable but condescending observation:

> Let us white people bend our every energy and apply every resource, public and private to educate ourselves and our children to treat the negro justly, honestly, and kindly. We are his superior, made so by God, and therefore being the stronger race, lend him our best efforts to help him along."[29]

In 1885, when Will Cook was ten years old, Samuel Clemens published *Adventures of Huckleberry Finn*. Many people in both the North and South at that time felt that blacks were sub-human, or at least a primitive, superstitious culture that could never be equal to whites.[30] Samuel Clemens foresaw and in a small way helped bring about the gradual acceptance of blacks as equals.

In the previously quoted exchange between Huck Finn and Aunt Sally about a steamship explosion, there was relief that no one was killed in the explosion, just a "negro."[31] When Huck observed Jim with his family, he expressed amazement at Jim's human-like qualities, "I do believe he cared just as much for his people as white folks does for their'n."[32]

Huck's epiphany finally came after his raft trip:

> "And got to thinking over our trip down the river, and I see Jim before me, all the time, in the day, and in the night-time, sometimes moonlight, sometimes storms, and we a floating along, talking, and singing, and laughing. But somehow I couldn't seem to strike no places to harden me against him, but only the other kind. I'd see him standing my watch on top of his'n, stead of calling me, so I could go on sleeping; and see him how glad he was when I come back out of the fog; and when I came to him again in the swamp, up there where the feud was, and such-like times; and would always call me honey, and pet me, and do every-

thing he could think of for me, and how good he always was; and at last I struck the time I saved him by telling the men we had smallpox aboard, and he was so grateful, and said I was the best friend old Jim ever had in the world."[33]

ON THE RAFT.

America eventually took the same path as Huck Finn in gradually coming to realize that blacks were equals. Clemens' voice of plain, unpretentious truth is no doubt the reason that Ernest Hemingway said all modern American literature comes from *Huckleberry Finn*.[34] Norman Mailer called it a transformative, extraordinary novel.[35]

Chapter Six

Elementary school

Blacks in America were on a steep climb up from a culture that had suffered centuries of no education and little chance for self-improvement. Fortunately, there were good men and women, black and white, who were determined to work for the betterment of former slaves and their descendants. Booker T. Washington, George Washington Carver, and many others saw education as the upward path for blacks. As they became more educated, men who had previously seen blacks as sub-human began to see them as human. George Washington Carver wrote to the head of the Tuskegee Institute, "You are teaching the southern white man to know us in a way that has never dawned upon him before."[36]

Churches attempted to be a healing force between the races. Nashville based David Lipscomb, writing about blacks, urged members of the Churches of Christ, "Treat them as devils, and you make demons of them; treat them with kindness as men, show confidence in them and trust them as men, and you make worthy men of them."[37] In Lake County, the Epworth League, an organization of Methodist young adults, conducted a program in Tiptonville in 1926 about "the negro in America." Among the topics covered was Christ's attitude toward race and class.[38]

That Job He's Got to Do

Abolitionists had a noble goal of a world where all men were free and equal, but they didn't have a clue of how to make it happen. Before the Civil War, ninety percent of blacks in America lived in the South. Fifty years later, ninety percent still lived in the South. "They were stuck between a white North that didn't want them and a white South that desperately needed them."[39]

By default, the day-to-day reality of implementing equality fell primarily to the tenant farmer. The relationships that some white owners had with their black tenants could be described as responsible paternalism, some could be called condescending paternalism, and some could best be described as ruthless exploitation.[40]

Tenants learned to get by the best ways they could. Most knew which farmers would squawk if an occasional chicken went missing and which ones would turn a blind eye. Tenants were also pretty realistic in their expectations, like the tenant who received a bottle of wine from the boss on Christmas Eve. On the day after Christmas, the boss asked him:

"Well, Uncle George, how was that wine?"

"It wuz jes rite."

"Just right, huh?" the boss replied.

"Yassuh," said the tenant, "if'n it had bin any bettah, you wouldn't uv give it to me, and if'n it had bin any wuss, I couldn't uv drunk it!"[41]

Attitudes of segregation were very slow to change. Most whites had a "crass race prejudice against the black race, few of whom had progressed much beyond slavery."[42] One time when some of

Chapter Six

Will Cook's cousins were working in the field, they sent their brother Max with the wagon to go to the house for water. At the well, Max filled two lard stands (about six gallons each) with

fresh drinking water, one for the whites and one for the blacks. As the wagon came back in the field, the men saw Max driving the wagon with the two lard stands in front of him and a bare foot in each lard stand. "Max! What are you doing?" they yelled, "You've got your feet in our water!" "Well," Max said, as if the answer ought to be self-evident, "my feet were HAHT."[43] It didn't take too long for their thirst to overcome their disgust and for them to take a drink. They might drink from a container that had their brother's foot in it, but they would never drink from the same bucket as a black man.

L.P. Hartley said, "The past is a foreign country; they do things differently there." Most blacks and whites of that time viewed the institutionalized segregation and discrimination as a way of life that, whether they agreed with it or not, they were powerless to change. The inertia of history, along with the threat of violence from some, meant that it would be decades before segregation began to change.

Many blacks accepted the way things were and tried to make the best of their place in the wide world. As one said, "I had to use the back door of the restaurant, but they charged me less for my food. I had to use the balcony at the theater, but I paid less for my ticket. I had to use the back door at the drug store, but the druggist never charged me anything."[44]

Unfortunately, in addition to the attitudes of segregation and white supremacy in America, there were outsiders actively working to sow hatred between the races. Karl Marx took a keen interest in the plight of former slaves. In them he saw the potential to create the class conflict he so desired to smash the bourgeoisie. Marx admired the Radical Republicans in the U.S. Congress such as Ben Wade of Kansas who called for redistribution of property.[45] Marx saw freedom and equality as ways to encourage blacks to migrate from agrarian jobs to depersonalized industrial employment where he believed they could be more easily manipulated.[46]

Communists like Karl Marx did not care about blacks other than as tools to create violence. Two years after the Russian Revolution, the summer of 1919 was called the Red Scare summer in America. Eight bombs went off in American cities, including one at the U.S. Attorney General's home. That summer was also the greatest period of interracial violence that America had ever witnessed. Twenty-six race riots occurred in cities like Chicago, Washington, Charleston, Knoxville, Nashville, and Omaha. In Chicago, twenty-three blacks and fifteen whites were killed.[47] In Elaine, Arkansas, there was a riot following reports that Bolsheviks had been organizing in the community. Officially, five whites and twenty blacks were killed there, but some reports said hundreds were killed.[48]

There were no riots in Lake County, but segregated justice was slow to change. Blacks who committed crimes or stepped out of line in any way could expect to be lynched. This news item from October 1900 described an incident in northern Lake County:

> About 11 o'clock one morning last week, a Russian Jew peddler was walking along the public road near Slough Landing, Lake County, when a negro named Williams came upon him and knocked him in the head with an iron coulter, and robbing him of his money, ran away, leaving his victim more dead than alive. He was soon found by friends and tenderly cared for, and while very painfully hurt, will likely recover. The negro's daring is shown by the fact that the deed was committed on the highway in broad daylight, within 300 yards of the residence of William Cates. A few hours after the crime was committed, the negro was arrested, carried to Tiptonville, and put in jail. The dastardly act

excited the indignation of the populace. The next night about 11 o'clock, a crowd of cool and determined men went to the jail, secured the keys from the jailer, pulled the negro from his cell, and carrying him about a half mile from town, hung him to the limb of an elm tree and quietly dispersed.[49]

Between 1901 and 1910, nine black men were lynched in Lake County – four for murder, three for rape, and two for fighting.[50] One of the murderers, Marshall Stanback, was completely unrepentant. His last words before he was hung were that he wished he could have killed more white men.[51]

Violence also occurred one-on-one. The relationships between planters and tenants varied widely, with some having close working relationships and some being antagonistic. Some planters felt it was in their best interest to keep the tenant always in debt to them, so they could not leave, a system referred to as peonage. This system sometimes led to violence.

In Drew, Mississippi, in December 1923, a black tenant shot his landowner who had been trying to collect a debt. *Negro World*, a newspaper that had wide circulation in the rural black community, praised the killing and said this type of action should be encouraged.[52] There may have been one tenant in Lake County, Tennessee, who took this advice to heart.

Three years later, there was a planter named Zellner Leech in the northern end of Lake County near Will Cook's farm. On January 23, 1927, one of his black tenants, Henry Walker, who was heavily in debt to Leech, threatened to leave town without paying his debts. When Leech rode up to the tenant house to prevent him from leaving, he was killed by a shotgun blast from Walker.[53] A manhunt ensued which covered the entire area for several days. Walker's body was eventually found in the bottoms between his house and Tiptonville. Some said he died of a heart attack from the exertions of flight; some said he died of exposure to the January cold, and some said he died of lead poisoning.

That Job He's Got to Do

There is often one person in a family who keeps alive memories that other people have forgotten.[54] Will Cook's grandson, Woody Cook, to whom this work is dedicated, set this author on a journey of discovery. According to Woody, there was a black man on Will Cook's farm in the 1920's who cursed in front of one of Will's daughters. The daughter told Will, and Will killed the man.[55]

There are many stories in history that, in spite of the fact that they were well documented at the time, are impossible to later sort out exactly what happened. With this story of Will Cook, there is no documentation at all. No newspaper stories have been found to confirm it. No law enforcement records apparently exist. Death records of black men who died violently are unfortunately plentiful.[56] It is impossible to know at this point whether the story is even true. If it is true, it is impossible to know the exact circumstances of how it may have transpired.

Will Cook is certainly innocent till proven guilty, and there is no evidence of a killing, but the numerous oral histories telling essentially the same story suggest that it did occur. There is another family account that says the man didn't just curse, but assaulted Will's daughter.[57] Given Will Cook's well-known temper,[58] it seems likely that if a killing did occur, it was an act of passion and not of pre-meditation.

"Small minds love to bring large news, and failing a load, will make one."[59] It would be easy to look at this story and say it was just another example of a racist who took the opportunity to kill a black man. It is the belief of this author, however, that this killing had little to do with race and much to do with honor. The main factor that race played was the lack of any investigation afterwards.

To try to understand Will Cook's motive, it is necessary for us to understand the role that honor plays in the lives of men.

Young men disagreeing on a point of honor.

7.
Honor and Truth

Honor can be a troublesome thing,
 but if one has it, one does not lightly yield it.

- Louis L'amour, *The Walking Drum*

In the spring of 1864, during the War Between the States, Grant set out to control the Shenandoah Valley by attacking Lee's flank. Their armies met near the town of New Market, Virginia. The corps of cadets from nearby Virginia Military Institute joined in the battle, and ten cadets gave their lives in the fighting.

Each year from 1887 to the present, VMI has honored those fallen cadets. The current corps stands in full dress review during roll call. Each squad and company reports the names of the fallen cadets who are absent from the ranks. The names pass forward by platoon to company and to the regimental commander, who reports to the commandant of cadets the names, "Atwill, Cabell, Crockett, Hartsfield, Haynes, Jefferson, Jones, McDowell, Stanard, Wheelwright." As each name is called, comes the reply, "Died on the field of honor, Sir."

Honor may be described as self-respect and respect from those who share similar values. It is generally associated with honesty and integrity, an independent self-sufficiency, a dominion over things within one's responsibility, and personal valor in defending those things. An honor not worth dying for is no honor at all. Just as obedience is the moral imperative of a boy, so honor is the moral imperative of a man.[1]

Integrity comes from the same root word as *integer*, meaning whole. Being a whole person who has principles and applies them in all aspects of life results in respect for self and for others. This is reflected in Shakespeare's excellent advice from the not-so-excellent Polonius:

> This above all – to thine own self be true,
> And it must follow as the night the day,
> Thou canst not then be false to any man.[2]

Honor is paid to those who, like the young men of Virginia Military Institute, stood for and defended the principles in which they believed. The northern boys who died fighting for their principles were honored with this tribute from Emerson:

> So nigh is grandeur to our dust,
> So near is God to man,
> When Duty whispers low, "Thou must,"
> The youth replies, "I can."[3]

Sir Francis Doyle paid tribute to the honor of the English soldier with these lines:

> Ay, tear his body limb from limb,
> Bring cord, or axe, or flame;
> He only knows, that not through *him*
> Shall England come to shame.[4]

Shakespeare's King Henry before the battle of Agincourt famously said,

> I am not covetous for gold,
> Nor care I who doth feed upon my cost,
> It yearns me not if men my garments wear;
> Such outward things dwell not in my desires;
> But if it be a sin to covet honor,
> I am the most offending soul alive.[5]

The desire for honor is hard-wired in us. The God who created us made us a little lower than the angels and crowned us with glory and honor.[6] The ancient Spartan mothers who told their sons to either come home *with* their shields or *on* them, the Knights of the Roundtable, the Japanese samurai, and the American military, among others, have all embraced the concept of death before dishonor.[7] The signers of the Declaration of

Independence pledged the most precious things they owned – their lives, their fortunes, and their sacred honor.

Aaron Burr - Alexander Hamilton duel

Honor, like any trait, can be used for good or for ill. Honor sometimes expressed itself in duels. In Alexander Hamilton's fatal duel with Aaron Burr, it is said he intentionally fired over the head of Vice President Burr, because preserving his honor was more important to him than preserving his life.

In later life when Andrew Jackson recalled his duel with Charles Dickinson, his account differed somewhat from contemporary accounts, but it illustrated his willingness to die to defend his honor. On being asked when in life he had been most frightened, Jackson replied:

> "It was, sir, when I fought the duel with Mr. Dickinson. In the first place, sir, I had no unkind feeling against Mr. Dickinson, and no disposition to injure a hair on his head. I had gone as far as an honorable man could go to avoid the

Chapter Seven

difficulty with Dickinson; he had not injured me, and therefore, I had no ground of complaint against him; my quarrel had been with his father-in-law, Col. Erwin. I knew Dickinson to be a brave, honorable gentlemen, and the best shot with the pistol I ever saw – far better than myself, for I was never an expert with that weapon. I knew that he could shoot quicker and truer than I could. I therefore went upon the ground expecting to be killed, and I owe the preservation of my life on that occasion to the fashions of the day, for I wore a coat with rolling collar and very full breasted, but fortunately for me, sir, I was organized with a very narrow chest. Dickinson's ball struck very near the center of my coat, and, while it scraped the breast bone, it did not enter the cavity of the chest. In an instant, under the impression that I was, perhaps, mortally wounded, and upon the impulse of the moment, I fired, and my antagonist fell – and no event in my life, sir, have I regretted so much."[8]

Charles Dickinson - Andrew Jackson duel

Social codes at the time saw "violence as an acceptable means of settling interpersonal disputes resulting from the defense of honor, person, or property."[9] In Lake County, Tennessee, the pursuit of honor led to several feuds. Mark Twain made fun of one of them in his book, *Life on the Mississippi*, saying that the feud was so old that the families had forgotten what it was about. Twain suggested that all the people in these two families had been killed because of some long-forgotten horse or cow.[10] The people involved in the feuds, however, remembered all too well the perceived dishonor done to a family member. One of the battles in the famous Watson-Darnall feud took place near the area where the Cook farm was later located, at a landing near Island 10 on board the steamship *Belle of Memphis*.[11]

A vigorus sense of honor was still alive in northwest Tennessee in the 1900's. Real or perceived threats to a woman's honor were met with deadly seriousness. In May of 1925 at Cates Landing near the Cook home, Richard Downing was dancing with the wife of a man named King. King shot Downing five times, killing him instantly.[12]

One local duel occurred on March 17, 1929. On that Sunday afternoon, Bill Cavett, age 45, of Tiptonville and Roy Parkerson, age 40, of Samburg had an argument after a poker game in Samburg and agreed to a duel in the old time manner. In the Reelfoot Lake version of *code duello*, they met outside, each with a pistol in his right hand. They locked their left hands together and on signal, commenced firing. Cavett received five bullets in his body and Parkerson two. Both men died.[13]

Men who took the law into their own hands did not see themselves as lawless. Somewhat like people today who believe in the use of force for self-defense, they saw themselves as acting where the law could not. They believed their actions were done "not to violate, but to vindicate the law."[14]

Chapter Seven

Law enforcement often saw no reason to get involved in duels or feuds. "A crime of passion in response to a family wrong was often treated with acquittal. If the law intervened at all, the penalty was often slight."[15]

Unlike heathen civilizations, where women were treated like property or of no importance, Western Civilization put a high value on how women were treated. "Fierce retaliation was therefore mandatory when a daughter, wife or mother had been dishonored."[16] Men saw it as their sacred duty to respond to any dishonoring of women. At a Georgia Baptist association in 1908, a resolution was offered denouncing "Night Riders, lynch law, and lawlessness in general." The moderator of the meeting opposed the resolution, proclaiming, "Not until my right hand forgets its cunning and my tongue cleaves to the roof of my mouth will I forget to protect the women, lynch law or no lynch law."[17]

Neighbors sometimes joined together to enforce justice. If a man was mistreating his wife, he might receive an intervention from a visiting party of neighbors. Typically, a whipping and a warning would be issued to encourage him to do the right thing and to avoid a castration on the return trip. A second visit was seldom necessary.[18]

We live in a fallen world where popular media today inflicts every sort of violent, vicious and vile influence on children. Some parents have completely given up even trying to protect their childrens' innocence. Some women as well as men now find it empowering and actually take pride in their ability to curse fluently. So it may be difficult to believe, but there was a time in America when women neither cursed nor tolerated cursing.

Even men of that day who were rough and violent did not curse in front of a lady or a child. In the presence of a dance-hall girl or a woman in a disorderly house, yes, but in front of a lady of quality or a child, never. Some small vestige of this remains today with people who will curse and then turn to a lady nearby and say, "Pardon my language."

It has been said that the Inuit language of the Arctic has a multitude of words for those frozen precipitations that other tongues call *snow*. Actually, the way that Inuits combine adjectives with nouns produces many words for almost everything. The point is still valid, however, that these people recognize more types of snow than people in temperate climes.[19] You could also say that Italians recognize many types of pasta that other people lump together as just noodles.

In somewhat the same way, modern people have many different words for offenses that earlier societies referred to collectively as *assault*. That is why a story that a man cursed in front of Will Cook's daughter is not in conflict with one that said a man assaulted Will Cook's daughter. Maybe a man forcibly laid hands upon a daughter; maybe he cursed in front of her. The point is that, to a man protecting his daughter's honor, there was no distinction whatsoever. In Will Cook's view, any man, black or white, who would commit one act, would commit the other.

"There are two kinds of injustice:" Cicero said, "the first is found in those who do an injury, the second in those who fail to protect another from injury when they can."[20] Will Cook was not going to fail to protect his daughter. Upon hearing that her innocence had been assaulted, Will likely was overcome with rage. If the offending party was close at hand, he would have been immediately confronted. Any such confrontation could quickly escalate to physical violence. Death, by means of whatever weapon or tool was at hand, or with bare hands, could easily ensue.

The Book of Exodus says, "He who strikes a man so that he die shall surely be put to death. However, if he did not lie in wait, but God delivered him into his hand, then I will appoint for you a place where he may flee."[21] Will Cook did *not* have to flee to a city of refuge. Lake County, the last frontier of Tennessee, *was* a place of refuge for those who defended family honor.

Chapter Seven

There is much we do not know about Will Cook. We do not know for sure if he killed a man. If he did, we do not know if he felt justified in his actions, if it was a situation that escalated out of control for which he was later penitent, or if it was just another job he had to do.

We *do* know that Will was a church going man. More importantly, we know that Will Cook does not have to answer to any of us for his actions. Like all of us, he will answer for himself when he stands before God.

The Good Book tells us that children are not responsible for their ancestor's sins. "The son shall not bear the guilt of the father, nor the father bear the guilt of the son."[22] Almighty God does tell us, though, that sin can have a persistent effect in families and nations. "For I, the Lord your God, am a jealous God, visiting the iniquities of the fathers upon the children to the third and fourth generations of those who hate me."[23] "Our fathers sinned and are no more, but we bear their iniquities."[24]

One way of judging a tree is by the fruit it produces. One way of judging a man is by his offspring. If we look at Will Cook through the lens of the children he produced, we do not see a racist or a murderer or an evil man. We see a man who, with his wife, raised a whole passel of young'uns who grew up to be people of honor and truth.

That Job He's Got to Do

Helen, Libby, and Joe Cook

Back Row L - R:
Kathleen Mae Cook, Dortha Richardson, Pauline Cook, Lillian Richardson.

Front Row L - R:
Malcolm Cook, L.D. Cook, Griffin Cook, Woodrow Cook, Russell Nell Richardson.

8.
A Two-Man Biscuit Pan

Be it ever so humble, there's no place like home.

- John Howard Payne, *Home, Sweet, Home*

A photograph taken about 1920 shows Will and Rachel's children sitting with some of their Richardson cousins on the front porch of their house. Will and Rachel's seventh child, Helen Frances Cook, who was born June 4, 1919, is not in the picture.

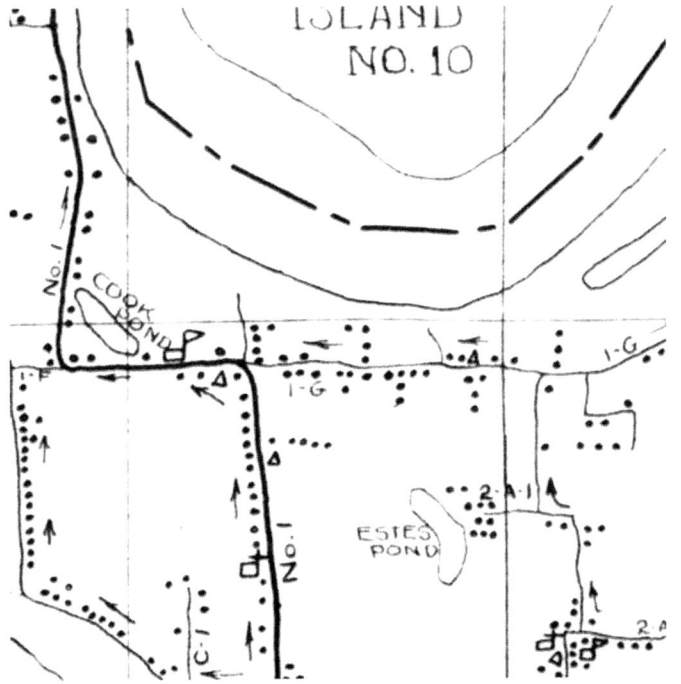

Houses, schools, stores, and churches in the Cooks' neighborhood

The house in the picture was built after the tornado blew away their old house. It is much like the typical tenant farmer houses that abounded in those days. Most of these are now gone. In the

Chapter Eight

early twentieth century there were seventy-five dwellings between the Cook home and the Kentucky state line.[1] Today there are only twelve newer homes. One Lake County tenant house that was preserved was the boyhood home of future country music star, Carl Perkins. That house is on display in Tiptonville today.

Carl Perkins' house of boyhood days

The children in the picture have possibly been in the field working and are now resting after lunch. Or perhaps they have been doing other chores. Maybe it is a Saturday, a day when men and mules didn't have to work as hard as usual. Maybe they are waiting to walk to the store in Cronanville, or maybe they will ride in the wagon to Bessie or to Tiptonville.

Tenant farmers not only struggled financially, but also with the constant threat of disease and death. The girl in the picture on the right hand of the front row was cousin Russell Nell Richardson. She died in 1927 at the age of fourteen from bronchial pneumonia and endocarditis. Nell's mother, Ludie Richardson, died in 1921 at age thirty-five of blood poisoning following a miscarriage. A twenty-two year old neighbor, Daisy Cook, a black housewife of Cronanville, died in 1916 of tuberculosis. There were few families not touched by death from tuberculosis, typhoid fever, smallpox, scarlet fever, malaria, polio, pneumonia, diphtheria, whooping cough, or infections at one time or another. The Bible's exhortation that life is only a vapor was readily apparent.[2]

The children learned early in life that there were jobs they had to do. Will Cook was of the generation that would issue orders to the children for the work to be done and would expect to be obeyed. The children were given age appropriate responsibilities and held accountable, receiving mild reprimands if they slacked off. Will didn't depend on reprimands, though. He would lead by example and would be the hardest worker on the farm. When Papa assigned a job, the child would be on it like a duck on a June bug, not out of fear, but from a desire to please Papa.

Libby feeding chickens

Shelling peas and snapping beans were good jobs for little fingers. Feeding the chickens and gathering eggs were also easy jobs for little ones. As they grew older, pumping water, bringing

Chapter Eight

in firewood for the cook stove, and feeding the milk cow would be important jobs. Churning the cream into butter would be a chore for some of the children. Some would help in the kitchen, and others would shell corn. Children would go into the woods in late spring to pick dewberries. In the fall after frost, they would collect pecans, walnuts, and hickory nuts.[3]

As needed, the children would be used in the cotton fields chopping, hoeing, and picking. The girls and women would help in the fields part of the day, leaving ahead of the men so they could prepare meals. The whole family would be employed in the garden to plant, water, hoe, and pick. Children learned to be productive members of the family. Child labor prepared them to become productive members of society when they were grown.

Children in Oklahoma picking cotton in 1916.

Older boys would help cut wood, and to fish and hunt for food. As soon as a boy was old enough to walk behind a plow, he was expected to begin doing a man's work. Indeed, the goal of any boy was to be accepted as a man, just as the girls wanted to be like their mother. A boy would receive ten cents for a whole day of plowing.[4] By the week's end, he would have enough money to purchase several things in town.

1924 Dime

That Job He's Got to Do

Tiptonville in the 1920s had five general stores, nine grocery stores, two drug stores, one motion picture theater, and a pool hall.[5] The four mile walk to Tiptonville was no step for a stepper, but coming back after dark would mean walking by the Cronanville cemetery. In the daytime the graveyard would be as dead as a doornail, but at night it would be easy to imagine noises coming from the graves of the Confederate soldiers. It would be easy to imagine some creature or thing rising out of the mists in the surrounding sloughs. A boy might imagine he heard something following him, but when he stopped to listen, it would stop. When he moved again, he could hear something move. When he sped up, he could hear the noise speed up. Soon, he would light out like a scalded dog the last mile to the house.

Free time for the boys sometimes consisted of exploring the world around them. Standing on the bank of the mighty Mississippi and looking at the Missouri shore a mile away, it would be easy to imagine that there was no way to get over there unless you were born over there.[6] Of course, for people who could pay, there were mule-powered and steam-powered and later petroleum-powered ferries across the river. Some of the boys did learn to navigate the powerful and dangerous currents of the river and

Chapter Eight

swim to the other shore, possibly stopping at one of the buoys to rest before plunging back into the swift current. Closer to home was the Cook pond, which provided boating in the summer and ice skating in the winter.

Boating on Cook Pond. Note telephone poles along levee in distance.

Everyone had to work hard, but life had a gentle, copacetic rhythm. Each person knew what was expected of him or her. All did their work by day and rested by night. When the work day was over, night would descend as soft and still as a blanket of cotton over the land. Occasionally, crickets and nocturnal animals would disturb the quiet, but most of the night was as quiet as a rabbit's dance. The humidity in summertime was an ever present force that would subside at night to just bearable levels. On occasions when the temperature and humidity did not relent, the day, as Harper Lee noted, "was twenty-four hours long, but seemed longer."7

That Job He's Got to Do

On Sunday all put on their best clothes and went to church. A half-mile to the north was Old Salem Methodist Church on John Cook's land.[8] A mile to the south was Jones Chapel Church of Christ in Cronanville. John R. Williams, a Church of Christ preacher from Marshall County, Tennessee, had moved to Hornbeak and begun preaching in Lake County.[9] He was said to have a keen intellect, a studious bent, a magnetic personality, and a zest for life.[10] When he came to Kentucky Bend to preach, about forty people joined the church.

John R. Williams

People all over the community were solicited for donations to build a building for Jones Chapel Church of Christ. Donations ranged from fifty cents to fifty dollars; John Cook contributed ten dollars. In 1912 the building was finished on the site of the old Cumberland Presbyterian Church in Cronanville. It held one service each week throughout the year. On Sunday morning the church yard would be full of wagons and mules. Baptizing was done across the levee in the river near Cates Landing or in one of the washout holes from the flood. Within three years there were one hundred fifty members.[11] Will's wife Rachel became a member of Jones Chapel Church of Christ in 1920.[12]

Chapter Eight

In the summer after crops were laid by, there would be a two-week revival at church with 2 p.m. and evening services. The building was lit with lanterns for the evening services.[13] Palm leaf fans were the only air conditioning on hot days and nights.

Will and Rachel's family was still growing with Joe Lafayette Cook born on August 25, 1921, Mary Elizabeth (Libby) Cook born June 21, 1923, and Gordon Lambert Cook born March 25, 1927. The nursery at church consisted of pallets on the floor around the preacher, and sometimes the members feared that the preacher would step on a baby.[14] Older children found church to be an opportunity for socializing. Norman Parks remembered getting to sit by Pauline Cook every night during one of the meetings.[15]

Lambert on tricycle

Unless it was a dire situation, no work would be done on Sunday except essential chores like cooking, milking the cow, pumping water, and bringing in firewood. After church and Sunday dinner, there might be neighbors who came by to visit. Perhaps Will might walk over the farm and inspect the crops or check on the other tenants. Sometimes there were Sunday afternoon baseball games nearby.

That Job He's Got to Do

Feeding a husband, eleven children, cousins, and any neighbor who dropped by, was a huge undertaking. Someone said that the biscuit pan at the Cook house was so big it took two people to get it out of the oven.[16]

A recipe for beaten biscuits at the time was:

> One quart flour, one-half cup butter or lard, one-half teaspoonful salt, scant teaspoonful baking powder. Make a stiff dough with one pint of cold sweetmilk, knead a little, then turn out on board and beat with a rolling pin for twenty minutes or one-half hour. Roll out one-half inch thick, cut in small cakes, prick with fork, and bake in moderate oven for about fifteen minutes.[17]

Along with hundreds of other duties, kitchen duty involved killing, scalding, plucking, singeing, and cutting up chickens to fry. During the summer there were vegetables to can. When it was time to harvest apples and peaches, some of the crop would be canned, and some sliced and put on the roof to dry in the hot sun.[18] At hog-killing time, there was much meat to be canned and salted down. Every week there was cleaning and ironing.

Farmers often kept a cow for milk and cream. A barn stall would have a feed trough with a stanchion so that when the cow began eating, the stanchion would keep her from backing out until the milking was done. A lantern could be set far enough away from the cow that she couldn't bother it, but the milk bucket had to be set right in front of the back legs, a prime spot for being kicked. A hobble with two loops would be placed around the back legs of the cow, keeping her from kicking. Sometimes these restraints would have a sharp point inside that would stick the cow's leg if she tried to kick.

Sometimes a stubborn cow would kick against these sharp points in spite of the pain. When the preacher read what Christ said to the rebellious Saul of Tarsus, "How hard it is to kick against the pricks,"[19] the farmer knew exactly what that meant. There was a lesson for hard-headed adults or children in cow hobbles.

Chapter Eight

Big Woody Cook, left, and C.B. Makin, right, holding 81 lb catfish.

Cleaning fish and fowl were important parts of feeding the family. There were always plenty of fish and ducks. On average during duck season there were a thousand ducks per day killed at Reelfoot.[20] There were so many ducks that "the roar of the tens of thousands of ducks and geese was deafening. When they rose from the water's surface into the sky, a cloud formed overhead darkening the earth."[21]

Lake boat

Reelfoot retained some of its frontier sensibilities long after the rest of the state became civilized. During most of Reelfoot's first century, there were no hunting limits and a seemingly limitless supply of ducks. "Sports" came from far away to be guided by local guides or "pushers," who pushed their pirogues along with poles. The Calhoun lake boats had double jointed paddles that allowed guides to row while facing forward. Guides often supplied live decoys. Female ducks (susies) were anchored so they could not fly far. Accompanied by their "gentleman friends," they lured unsuspecting wild ducks to come close. Live decoys were eventually outlawed, and limits were gradually reduced to sustainable levels.

Donald V. Sabin photo, pemission of Tenn. State Library & Archives.

The boys learned to be good shots; duck hunting was no place for someone who couldn't hit the broad side of a barn. One Samburg hunter, "Slingshot" Charley Taylor, became nationally famous for his ability to shoot ducks out of the sky using a slingshot.

The game warden was never "one to trouble himself over frequent violations of state and local laws by the lake people."[22] The lake people, in turn, did not openly flout the game and fish laws but always made sure they didn't get caught. Locals were somewhat like a later show called *The Dukes of Hazzard* in that they did "just a little bit more than the law allows."[23]

Sometimes they did a *lot* more than the law allows. Market hunters would kill hundreds of ducks, ice or salt them down in barrels, and sell them to big city markets for a dollar each. This practice did not completely end until the Federal "ducklegger" trials of the 1950's. Some of Will's sons earned money this way. One of Will's sons, L.D., served as game warden for awhile.

Your Game And Fish Officer

(This is the fifth in a series of articles dealing with all of West Tennessee's game and fish officers.)

L. D. Cook, law enforcement supervisor for District 12, which includes Lake, Crockett, Dyer, Obion, Carroll, Henry, Gibson and Weakley Counties, began his work with the Tennessee Game and Fish Commission in 1949.

His first job was junior area manager in the Reelfoot Lake area. He served in that capacity until 1955 when he was promoted to district law enforcement supervisor.

Prior to working with the commission, Cook was in the Army four years. After World War II, he returned to Tiptonville, Tenn., where he farmed until he decided conservation work was for him.

Cook and his wife reside at 934 Church Street in Tiptonville.

L. D. Cook

L.D. Cook as game warden

That Job He's Got to Do

There was at least one time when Will's sons stayed within the legal limits, when they hunted on a Mississippi River island, as recounted by Griffin:

> My friend Willis Bashears had never been on a real hunt. When he came up from Augusta, Ga., to Tiptonville, Tenn., for a visit one December day in 1942, my brother Woody Cook and I made him a rash promise. "Come duck hunting and we'll show you where to get the limit as fast as you can pull the trigger," we said. Although we were up early for the 12 mile trip to our favorite hunting ground, it looked for a while as if we might eat, not duck, but those boasting words. Our motorboat developed engine trouble; we had to drive part way and walk the rest; it was late in the day – 1:30 p.m. – when we arrived; and we could carry only seven decoys. A chilling wind kicked up waves in the river. The ducks headed for a calm pocket. We hustled to build a blind. The deadline on duck hunting was only a few hours off. But the mallards were with us. They started coming in like fighter planes out of gas. The three of us began firing – and hitting. There wasn't even time to pick up our kill because the ducks kept coming. This is rare; usually they won't approach where dead ducks are in the water. Within an hour we had our limit, 30 ducks. It was one of the few times my brother and I were able to back up our tall tales of good hunting in Lake County. Bashears went home still marveling that we delivered on the ducks.[24]

A recipe for roast duck at the time said:

> Boil duck, adding one onion, a little vinegar, salt sage and pepper. Boil one hour. Make dressing of stale bread, highly seasoned with sage, salt, and pepper. Moisten dressing with the liquid in which the duck is boiled and add some beaten egg. Stuff the duck, lay strips of salt bacon on breast, having previously dredged with flour, salt and pepper. Boil down the liquid in which the duck is boiled, and baste with it as duck bakes. Remove slices of pork half an hour before duck is done.[25]

Chapter Eight

The nearby Cronanville school provided education for the children. McGuffey's Readers and Blue-Back spelling books were important parts of the curriculum.[26] There were about ninety students in ten grades with two teachers providing classes, daily singing, physical education, and hot food to supplement whatever the child brought from home.[27] One day the teachers might serve potato soup, another day spaghetti, and on another stewed fruit.

The boys' basketball team reported one week that there were two broken noses, one broken ankle, one split lip, one smashed eye, and two broken fingers.[28] (This style of basketball seems to have carried on in one of Will's grandsons, who once executed a perfect tackle on an opposing basketball player!)[29] A third of the students would leave school in May to chop cotton and again in October to pick.[30]

After ten years of fairly stable growing conditions, the flood of 1927 struck. Heavy rains in March and April produced large flooded areas. Lightning storms, hailstorms, windstorms, and unseasonably cold weather added to the miseries. When the flood waters finally subsided, it was too late to plant cotton.

Griffin, Woodrow, Malcolm, and L.D.

That Job He's Got to Do

The early Twentieth Century was a time of technological advancement in rural America. Telephone lines were installed and businesses began getting telephones. Later, electric poles and electricity would come to these same places. Farmers were interested in practical technology. Telephones and light bulbs were novelties, but a tool or an engine which made work easier was considered as handy as a pocket on a shirt.

The 1920's saw many households in America getting a radio set for the first time, usually powered with large batteries. Listening to the St. Louis Cardinals on KMOX or the Grand Ole Opry on WSM became a treat in well-to-do households. The U.S. Census of 1930 asked each household if it had a radio. Neither Will Cook's house nor any of his nearby neighbors indicated on the census that they owned a radio. Maybe nobody in that area thought it was any business of the government to count radios. More likely, the Cooks found their entertainment in hunting, fishing, sports, and exploring the countryside. Will Cook didn't have time or money for unproductive frivolities like radios.

Will and Rachel's oldest child, Pauline, graduated from Tiptonville High School in 1928. At a time when most women did not venture beyond their rural hometowns, sisters Pauline and Kathleen moved one hundred miles south to Memphis where they found employment with Sears, Roebuck and Company. Pauline and Kathleen were both smart and well-liked. One of Kathleen's high school mementos was a note in Latin that translated, "I will always love you. Your friend, Richard Griffin."

The year 1930 was a terrible year. There was no rain for one hundred days between May and August. Farmers tried to mulch their crops to keep what little moisture they had, but to no avail.[31] Crops produced little that year. Will Cook's birthday in October was going to be a happy break from the year's problems, but a flat tire and a drunk driver brought disaster instead.

Chapter Eight

America has a complex history of trying to regulate alcoholic beverages, beginning with the Whiskey Rebellion of 1791. Americans originally took a libertarian view of alcohol, often believing that the individual was the best person to decide the issue. Tennessee historian Robert White noted the prevalence of alcohol in the state's early days; "Whiskey was used as a preventative of disease. It was regarded as a necessary beverage by the frontiersman. A log cabin could not be put up, a field of wheat could not be cut down, nor could there be a log-rolling, a husking bee, a wedding, or even a funeral without the aid of alcohol."[32]

Many people in the Reelfoot area were not opposed to some occasional "over the levee water," as the land between the levee and the river was sometimes used for hiding stills. The islands in the lake were also convenient places for those who wanted to do a little home brewing away from the prying eyes of revenuers.

The innocent wives and children, however, who suffered at the hands of drunken husbands and fathers, caused many people in America to change their minds about alcohol. Groups like the Women's Christian Temperance Union and individuals like Carrie Nation were influential in promoting Prohibition, the Eighteenth Amendment to the Constitution, which banned the production and sale of alcohol beginning in 1920.

Once alcohol was banned, unintended consequences began to appear. Organized crime increased as gangsters like Machine Gun Kelly of Memphis made money bootlegging. Another consequence was that, instead of drinking at home, people more frequently would go to joints where alcohol was available. Once there, they would over indulge and then get on the roadway.

Pauline and Kathleen Cook were being driven home from Memphis by Will Cook on Friday, October 25, 1930, to celebrate his fifty-sixth birthday the next day. As you travel north from Memphis through Dyer County, Tennessee, the road descends from some low-lying hills to the flat plain where the community of Bogota (bō-gŏt'-uh) is located. It was here on Highway 78 that Will's car suffered a flat tire. Flat tires were not uncommon, and drivers often carried more than one spare. On this day, according to the *Lake County Banner*:

> "... the two girls were standing behind the car while Mr. Cook fixed it. Seeing a car approaching at an extremely high rate of speed evidently headed directly at their stopped car, the girls jumped. Miss Kathleen ran clear down into the ditch – the oncoming car also swung off into the ditch behind her, caught and struck her, her body being thrown clear up against the windshield and carried several feet before she fell off."[33]

The car, driven by Odie Morris of Bogota, with passengers Robert Davis and Milton Bennett, at first stopped when the car stalled. Will Cook, with his dying daughter in his arms, pleaded with them to call an ambulance in Bogota, but instead they restarted the car and sped away. When Will finally reached Baird Brewer Hospital in Dyersburg, twenty-one year old Kathleen was pronounced dead. Her death certificate says she died instantly of a fractured skull.

Kathleen Cook

**Left to Right: L.D., Helen, Griffin, Pauline, Malcolm, & Woody.
Front Left to Right: Lambert, Libby, & Joe.**

That Job He's Got to Do

Rachel and Will

Chapter Eight

Odie Morris was jailed on charges of murder and driving-while-intoxicated. The Dyer County grand jury indicted him November 6 on a charge of involuntary manslaughter and released him on bond. On February 27, 1931, he was convicted and sentenced to eleven months and twenty-nine days in the county workhouse. Then four days later on March 2, he was released on a $750 bond, pending an appeal to the Tennessee Supreme Court. On October 19, 1932, the case was returned to Dyer County after being reversed and remanded by the Court of Criminal Appeals in Jackson. Morris was retried, found not guilty, and released.[34] He had served a total of thirteen days in jail for killing Kathleen Cook. The next year, the Twenty-first Amendment was passed which repealed Prohibition.

Rachel and Will

Will and Rachel Cook's twelfth baby was born when Rachel was forty-three years old and suffering from high blood pressure.[35] There was little treatment for hypertension in those days, even for the wealthy. Franklin D. Roosevelt suffered with it through much of his presidency. During the Yalta conference Roosevelt's blood pressure was 250 over 150, and just before he died, it was 350 over 195.

On a visit to the doctor shortly before the baby was born, Rachel came out crying.[36] No doubt the doctor had warned what might happen. Rachel delivered a healthy baby boy, but just two and a half hours later, she died of postpartum hemorrhaging. The baby was named R E in her memory. Rachel Emma Hammer, who was born in Grainger County, Tennessee, and married Will Cook in Carroll County, Tennessee, died in Lake County, Tennessee, November 17, 1931.

After her mother died, Pauline gave up a promising future in Memphis to return home and raise her younger brothers and sisters: L.D., age fifteen, Helen, age twelve, Joe, age ten, Libby, age eight, Lambert, age four, and baby R E. In 1939, Pauline married Harper Peacock, and they had a wonderful flower shop in Tiptonville for many years. Several of the other children worked at local businesses such as Markham Drug Store and Boyette's Restaurant.

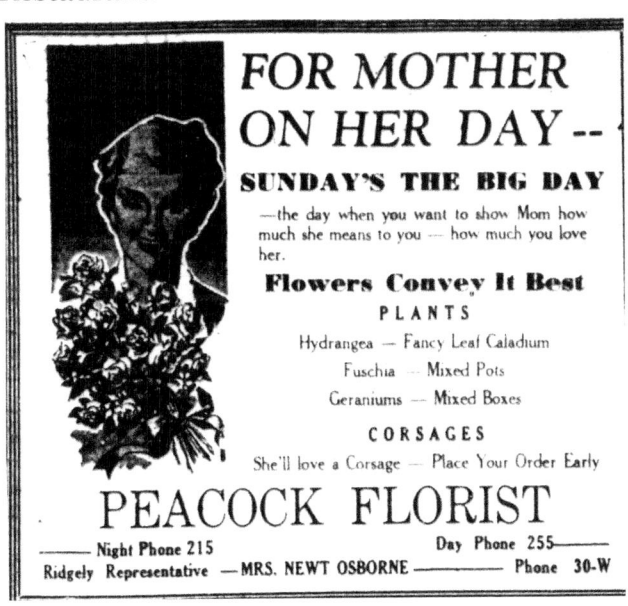

FOR MOTHER
ON HER DAY --

SUNDAY'S THE BIG DAY

—the day when you want to show Mom how much she means to you — how much you love her.

Flowers Convey It Best

PLANTS

Hydrangea — Fancy Leaf Caladium

Fuschia — Mixed Pots

Geraniums — Mixed Boxes

CORSAGES

She'll love a Corsage — Place Your Order Early

PEACOCK FLORIST

—— Night Phone 215   Day Phone 255——

Ridgely Representative —MRS. NEWT OSBORNE —— Phone 30-W

Chapter Eight

All of Will and Rachel's boys served their country in one way or another. Malcolm served with the U.S. Marines on Guadalcanal, New Guinea, Peleliu, and Iwo Jima. In one island battle, so many officers were killed and wounded that Gunnery Sergeant Cook became the ranking Marine.[37]

L.D. served in the U.S. Army Signal Corps in the Pacific. Lambert served in the U.S. Navy on a sub tender. R E served in the U.S. Air Force as a B-29 gunner. Woody and Joe served in the Tennessee State Guard. Griffin served in the Civilian Conservation Corps at Ft. Oglethorpe, Georgia, and then in the war defense industry in Lewisburg, Tennessee. Helen also served in the war defense industry in Memphis. Instead of Rosie the Riveter, she was affectionately known in the family as Helen the Welder.

Helen the Welder

Will's children all went farther in school than their father, most of them finishing high school. A few went to technical schools. Lambert had the distinction of being the first member of his family to go to college, attending Harding College in Searcy. Arkansas.

That Job He's Got to Do

Some of Will and Rachel's offspring were as independent as a hog on ice, but all ten of the surviving children became productive, moral, and kind citizens who worked, created, built, and made the world a better place. All had kindness and respect for others, black or white. One, for example, found out about a large black family whose children needed shoes, but couldn't afford them.[38] New shoes and several other things were done to help this family.

Will and Rachel's children all married, though not young. Woody, Griffin, and Malcolm all married in the same year - 1940. The average marriage age of the bunch was twenty-eight, with Lambert marrying at twenty-one and L.D. at thirty-six. None of the marriages ended in divorce. Twenty-one grandchildren were produced.

Biscuit pan made by Helen the Welder

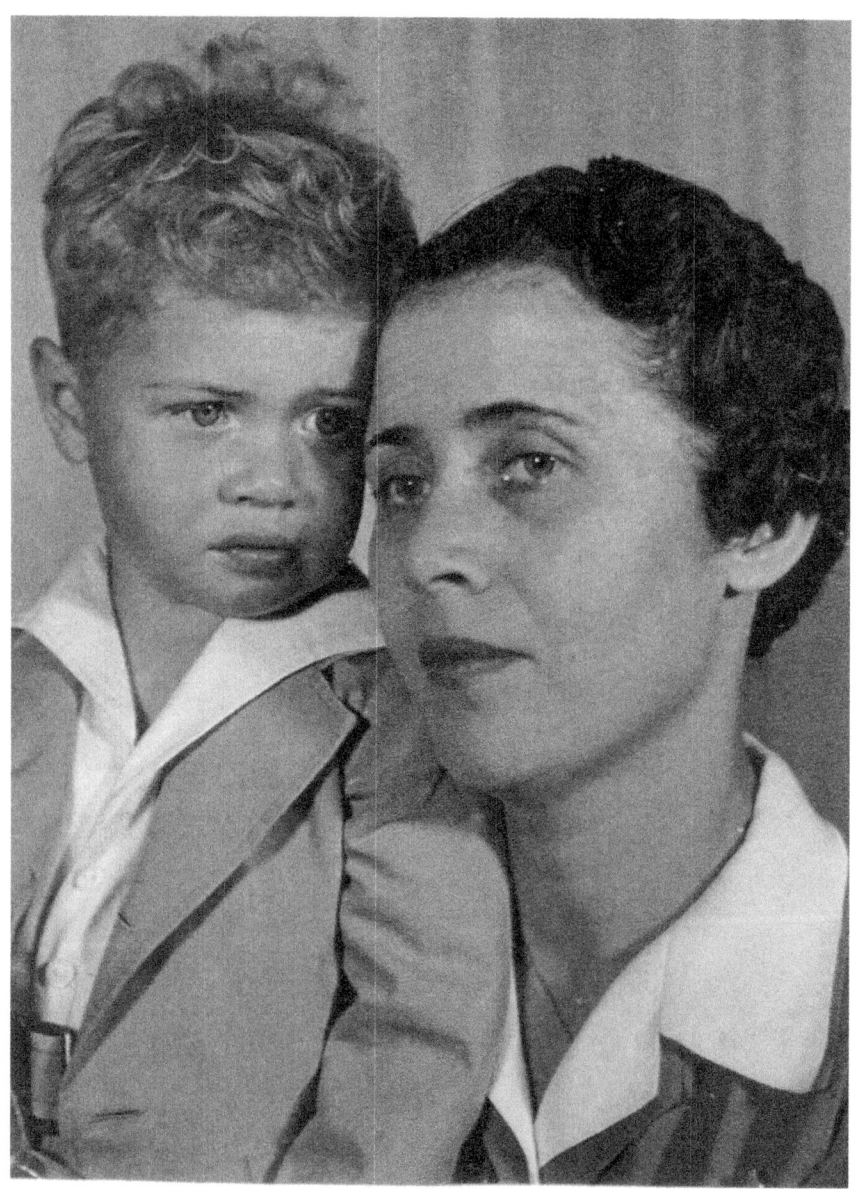

Pauline with Curry

That Job He's Got to Do

Kathleen Mae

Woodrow "Big Woody"

That Job He's Got to Do

Griffin with Claire

Chapter Eight

Malcolm with Ruth and Jim

That Job He's Got to Do

L.D.

Chapter Eight

Helen

That Job He's Got to Do

Joe

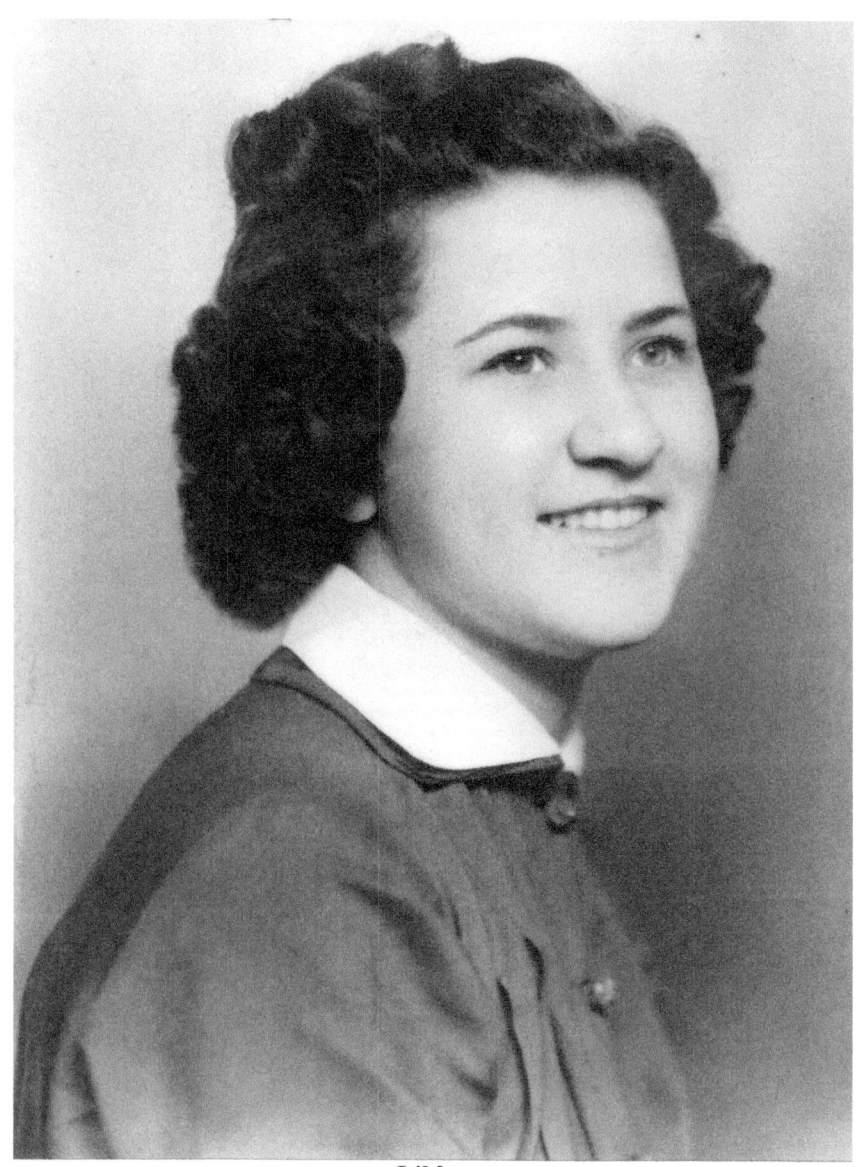

Libby

That Job He's Got to Do

Lambert

Chapter Eight

R E

That Job He's Got to Do

Helen, Griffin, Pauline, R E, and Lambert, June 29, 1991

Family reunion in June 1993.

Sunset over the Mighty Mississippi, west of Tiptonville.

9.
The Next Job

Ah gits weary an' sick of tryin'
Ah'm tired of livin' an skeered of dyin'
But ol' man river
He jes' keeps rollin' along.

  - Oscar Hammerstein II, *Ol' Man River*

For many Lake County residents, the Great Depression did not have a huge impact. As county historian Abigail Hyde said, "Before the Depression we had nothing; during the Depression we had nothing, and after the Depression we had nothing."[1] For some people who did struggle, the Roosevelt farm programs like the Agricultural Adjustment Act (AAA) of 1933 were welcomed as a life-preserver. Farmers who accepted it would rent about a third of their land to the government. This land could not be used for cash crops.[2]

However, many people across the country believed that, while millions of people were hungry, a government program that paid farmers to kill baby pigs and plow up crops was inherently evil. Paying people not to work also violated the basic, biblical truth that those who won't work shouldn't eat.[3] Sharecroppers were hurt by the farm program, because farmers didn't need as many workers when they weren't raising as many crops.

Groups like the Corn Belt Liberty League in Illinois fought a losing battle in trying to stop the AAA. In Lake County, some people saw the AAA as a dependency that would be "a rope around your neck" or "a snake that would bite you."[4] When the AAA men came to Will Cook's farm, he convinced them to travel elsewhere by

AAA man

brandishing the business end of a shotgun.[5]

The Depression meant lower prices for cash crops like cotton. In lean years, farmers were sometimes forced to rely on credit from the local store until harvest. Someone who ate dinner with the Cooks once commented about the meal, "I don't know if it was all paid for, but it was all good!"[6] Will Cook *did* pay his bills, though. Norman Parks, whose sister Maude operated a store, noted that during the lean year of 1934, Will Cook was one of those who had paid off his account at the store.[7]

Flooded farmland near Bessie, 1937.

January of 1937 brought more flooding to Lake County. Sleet storms had downed many phone lines, making it difficult to call Cairo, Illinois, for updates. Local rumors suggested that people from Missouri were coming to the Tennessee side to dynamite the levees. Several local people stood guard along the levees.

SCHOOL HOUSE DESTROYED BY FLOOD AT BESSIE

The local newspaper reported that no further flooding was expected, but on February 1, 1937, at 10:13 a.m., the river broke through the levee protecting the village of Bessie. No lives were lost, but the once bustling little community of Bessie was flattened. It was never rebuilt.

On March 15, 1938, the Cook family spotted a tornado headed their way. For a family who had once had their house blown away and many family members injured, it must have been a horrifying sight. Although the funnel appeared to be traveling directly up the river, it was actually a few miles west of the river. There was some destruction in Blytheville, Arkansas, but none in Lake County.[8]

John Cook moved into Tiptonville after the flood of 1937, but on May 5, 1938, he was "stricken with apoplexy" (suffered a stroke), fell into a coma, and died two weeks later.[9] At the beginning of the twentieth century, most landowners in Lake County lived on the land they farmed. By the end of that same century, however, most of the landowners were either widows or absentee owners. At John's death, Josie Cook became both widow and absentee landowner.

Will Cook had always enjoyed a good relationship with his brother John. Josie Cook was a person who was frequently mentioned on the society page of the local paper.[10] Perhaps Will thought she was too highfalutin for them to gee-haw together. Or perhaps the business relationship was changed by Josie. Whatever the reason, Will Cook retired at age 63 from a life of farming and moved to town.

In town, Will dressed the part of a man who had retired from hard work, wearing a suit and hat almost everywhere he went. Still there were always jobs to do. Will raised a garden and did handyman jobs. He was not one who was going to retire and get as fat as a town dog.

Will and Lambert

Chapter Nine

Will typically walked wherever he went. Sometimes, he might sit downtown and reminisce with old friends like Syl Sutton.[11] A good knife and a whittling stick may have been involved. During the war, there would have been much talk about Will's sons and other local boys who were involved in the conflict. After the war, President Truman came to town, staying two days at Linda Lodge near the lake and riding in a parade through town. Will attended football games and school activities like father-son banquets.[12]

Like several of his brothers before him, Will's son Joe was on the high school football team. R E and Lambert, the youngest sons, enjoyed the company of other boys in town. There were pecans to gather until the owner of the tree ran the boys off. There were nearby watermelon patches to raid. One time, the boys were full of daring. They drove beside a truck that was slowly driving up the levee, and helped themselves to a few watermelons from the moving truck.

R E holding Curry at Walnut Street house.

The Peacock house at 224 Walnut Street where Papa or Goggy (short for *grandfather*) lived was a welcoming place where friends or family might drop by anytime for a visit. An extra bed could always be found for company. Papa was always the first up in the morning, starting the fire in the cookstove and making coffee. Will's daughter-in-law Mary noted that Papa would often be found in the evening sitting in the dark at the house.[13] When one was raised to work from can to can't, it was second nature to function in whatever light was available and to accept the dark as a natural part of the day.

That Job He's Got to Do

Going fishing and hunting with grandson Curry and letting him help in the garden were welcome pastimes. Papa took at least one trip to Lewisburg, Tennessee, to visit son Griffin, taking Curry on the train to Nashville, where Griffin met them.[14]

The neighborhood boys were in the yard one day playing ball and evidently getting a little too noisy. Grandson David remembers Papa yelling out the window for them to get quiet.[15] Maybe Papa's health was beginning to decline and he couldn't take the commotion, or maybe he was just trying to take a nap. There was no question, however, that Papa would be obeyed. The boys got quiet.

Papa was not a social drinker, but neither was he a teetotaler. He bought three bottles of beer each week and put them in the icebox. He would space these out through the week, drinking them for better digestion.[16]

Will's daughter-in-law was at the house one day, and the talk turned to a neighbor who lately seemed to be wearing a serious expression.[17] Papa said, "He's worried about that job he's got to do." Claire, not understanding, thought perhaps he meant a farming job or a handyman job. "What job is that?" she asked. In his deep voice Papa replied, "He's got to DIE!"

On his last day, Papa completed at least a couple of jobs, fixing the roof and working in the garden. His grandchildren were a source of amusement for him. On his last night, as he was heading upstairs, two of his granddaughters were fussing about something. Papa just shook his head and said, "Kassie and Sissy got into a spat."[18]

The church song "Work for the Night is Coming" says, "Fill brightest hours with labor; rest comes sure and soon." Will Cook had filled his brightest hours with labor and was ready for his rest. He lived so that he could approach that job he had to do "Like one who wraps the drapery of his couch about him and lies down to pleasant dreams."[19]

Chapter Nine

William Lafayette Cook completed his last job on earth on Tuesday, May 24, 1949, passing quietly in his sleep from a massive heart attack at age seventy-four. His youngest son, who had been sleeping in the same room, didn't notice anything until he came downstairs the next morning and saw that Papa wasn't sitting in his chair. Pauline discovered her father's body in bed, and told the family.[20]

The funeral was held on May 26 at the Tiptonville Church of Christ with Homer Royster conducting the service.[21] Burial was in Tiptonville City Cemetery. As befitting the father of a florist, and a man who was well respected in the community, there were lots of flowers.

Will Cook's life, from growing up on a farm until he completed "that job he's got to do," was a life of action and accomplishment. He left little in the way of material possessions, but he left behind valuable lessons for us all.

Will Cook's grave, Tiptonville city cemetery.

That Job He's Got to Do

Reelfoot Lake eagle,
courtesy of Debbie Southerland Rogers and Tony Rogers.

Will Cook

10.
Knowing What to Throw Away,
and Knowing What to Keep

Every moment is a window on all time.

- Thomas Wolfe, *Look Homeward, Angel*

The gamblers who made their living playing cards on the Mississippi riverboats knew that every hand was a winner or every hand was a loser, depending on how it was played. Knowing what to throw away and knowing what to keep were critical.[1] So it is with remembering the life of William Lafayette Cook.

Riverboat gamblers

Ralph Waldo Emerson's statement that "Society never advances" is not true in the absolute. Society does advance. Emerson was correct, however, that there are always things gained and things lost. One only need look to modern society to see that gains in technology are measured against losses in basic morality.

When Emerson spoke of society not advancing, he was thinking of the New Zealand aborigines, and how a modern American

Chapter Ten

would have just as much trouble surviving in their world as the aborigine would have surviving in New York. So it is that many people today would have trouble surviving in the world of Will Cook. The physical labor and the lack of creature comforts would be more than some people could endure. Modern society has produced many people who wouldn't work in a pie factory, much less do the back-breaking work of a tenant farmer.

Will Cook's life was one of hard work, not necessarily because he liked hard work, but because he took responsibility for himself and for those in his care. Western civilization has risen to great heights partly because of the Judeo-Christian values that all people are created equal and that all are responsible for their actions. When a man practices righteousness, he should be rewarded, and when he does evil, he should pay for it.

Responsibility also involves keeping your word. In today's world, there are many slips 'twixt the cup and the lip, and a man's reliability often changes with the rising and setting of the sun. Men like Will didn't make rash promises or commitments they could not keep. When they gave their word, you knew it was good, and that they would fulfill their responsibilities.

> **"**To ride, shoot straight, and speak the truth—
> This was the ancient Law of Youth.
> Old times are past, old days are done;
> But the Law runs true, O little son!**"**
>
> —Charles T. Davis

Charles T. Davis poem, Sturm Ruger and Co. ad.

Ancient Chinese civilizations taught their sons "to ride, shoot straight, and speak the truth." Methods of riding and shooting may have changed, but there is still a need for skill, a steady hand, and most of all, the truth. As the patriarch Job said in the depths of his grief, "as long as breath is in me, and the spirit of God is in my nostrils, my lips will not speak falsehood, and my tongue will not utter deceit."[2]

Truth requires work. Not just accepting whatever one is told, but weighing it against the principles in which one believes, and connecting it in a consistent manner to all parts of life (to thine own self be true) is the responsibility of all who would be truthful.

Responsibility requires commitment. A favorite quote of the fickle, impatient modern world says that doing the same thing over and over again and expecting different results is insanity. Men and women of a nobler generation knew that doing the right thing over and over was not insanity. It was called perseverance and would eventually bring the right results.

I. PERSEVERANCE.

Chapter Ten

Race relations have come a long way since Will Cook's time, and they still have a long way to go. Just as they did in Will Cook's time, racists on one side and communists on the other side work against freedom for all. Communists like those at the Highlander Folk School[3] in Tennessee have not been interested in helping blacks, but in using them.

A favorite tactic of communists is hijacking other people's movements, which is what happened in the Russian revolution and many other places. Communists give the appearance of promoting civil rights when actually they are promoting civil conflict. Roy Blount, Jr. noted that, at the 1967 Vanderbilt University symposium featuring speakers such as Stokely Carmichael, "Stokely gave a liberal, intellectual speech to us mostly white folks and then went over to Nashville's black colleges, told them to kill Whitey, started a riot, and left town."[4]

One hindrance to equality in America that communists have promoted is the identity movement. Each person should be proud of his culture, but when that becomes more important than your identity as a Christian, as a father, as a husband or as a citizen, it prevents you from being your best at any of those things. Identity has been used to create a sense of false victimhood. When the most important thing to you is your superficial identity, every problem in life looks like prejudice.

Tower of Babel

Divisions between men first began when they began to build a great tower that would reach the heavens.[5] People of all colors and types are wise when they remember the lesson of Babel, that the sin of pride causes divisions in mankind. The only identity that matters is that we are all created in God's image.[6]

Thankfully, people today have come a long way toward accepting all people as God's children. The Good Book tells us,

That Job He's Got to Do

"He has made of one blood every nation of men" - Acts 17:26. "There is neither Jew nor Greek, slave nor free, male nor female, but all are one in Christ" - Galatians 3:28.

Will Cook probably granted friendship and equality on a case-by-case basis. If a man lived right and treated him right, he likely accepted him as a friend. Will lived much of his life with the equalizing effect of poverty, where everyone black and white had a common struggle to survive. Most people of Will's day, however, saw blacks as an inferior race. That is one of the things from Will Cook's time that we can and should leave in the past.

One thing from Will Cook's life that we should keep is a distrust of big government. An unfortunate consequence of the American Civil War was a concentration of power in Washington, D.C. The proliferation of government programs and agencies in Will Cook's time led many people to distrust anyone who said, "I'm from the government, and I'm here to help." We may not need to run the government agents off with a shotgun, as Will did, but we should be wary of the rope around our necks that government becomes.

Another consequence of the Civil War was the conversion of the South from an agrarian to an industrialized society. Will Cook was a man who never wavered from his connection to the land. He knew the soil. He knew the plants and animals that lived on the land. He knew the weather above it. Most importantly, he knew the basic truths of life seen by those who live close to the land. He knew how precious life was, and how easily the weeds would choke it out. He understood the necessity of wisely using the resources that God has given. When the preacher spoke about reaping what you sow, Will understood the lesson completely. Only one of Will's children (L.D.) became a farmer, but many of his children stayed connected to the land through gardening or hunting or fishing or growing flowers.

Some people today reject all value system as authoritarian and oppressive. Ironically, their personal values often come from God even though they don't recognize God. Just as anyone who follows the days of the week is consciously or unconsciously recognizing the God who created the world in six days and rested on the seventh, so anyone who recognizes the values of being kind to others, loving your family, protecting children, honoring ancestors, and having personal integrity, is consciously or unconsciously recognizing the God who gave those precepts. The wise man said that there is nothing new under the sun.[7] The ancient landmarks[8] and the old paths[9] are guides from the past that we should keep.

Will and Rachel Cook knew instinctively what some in modern society deny, that all life is precious. Most mothers of that day saw a baby as a gift, not an inconvenience. If a mother was not ready for a baby, she might take it to a place like the Tennessee Children's Home Society in Memphis, where the worst thing that might happen was that the baby would be sold to a loving couple who desperately wanted a child.[10] Tragically, in modern society some women have lost the mothering instinct and believe it is their sacred right to chop up the baby and sell the parts to the highest bidder.

From the Garden of Eden to the present, sin has been the destroyer of anything good, as Kipling noted:

That Job He's Got to Do

On the first Feminian Sandstones,
we were promised the Fuller Life,
(Which started by loving our neighbor,
and ended with loving his wife)
Till our women had no more children,
and the men lost reason and faith,
And the gods of the copybook headings said:
"The Wages of Sin is Death."[11]

Will and Rachel Cook also knew instinctively what many in modern society have willingly forgotten, that the family is the basic unit of civilization. Good wives and mothers were cherished then and not denigrated. Mothers saw a house full of boys and girls as a treasure better than gold. As author C.S. Lewis said, "The housewife's work ... is surely in reality the most important work in the world ... it is the one for which all others exist."[12] Will and Rachel knew that the hand that rocks the cradle rules the world.

With apologies to Kipling:[13]

Now this is the law of the family,
As old and as true as the sky.
And the family that keeps it may prosper,
But the family that breaks it must die.
The law, like the sun in the heavens,
Shines true wherever we roam:
The strength of the Home is the Woman,
And the strength of the Woman is Home!

Good men saw it as their duty, honor, and privilege to protect and provide for the home. As author Robert Heinlein said, "Every human culture is based on 'Women and children first' – and any attempt to do it any other way leads quickly to extinction."[14] Good fathers are important not only to protect and provide, but to set each family member free to be whomever he or she should be. Certainly many good homes exist with only one parent, but the best way is the way that God designed it.[15] That is something from the life of Will and Rachel Cook that we should keep.

Chapter Ten

Will Cook's mother died at age thirty-two. His wife died at age forty-three. One thing we can gladly leave in the past is short life expectancies. Thanks to American health care, Will's daughters and daughters-in-law lived longer lives than did previous generations.

From the Lake County Banner, July 18, 1947.

One thing we have kept from Will Cook's time that should be thrown away is allowing intoxicated people to slaughter people on our highways with little consequence. The young life of Kathleen Cook was taken away, and the guilty man received only a slap on the wrist. Tragically, it still happens today.

Bugs & Sam
©**Warner Brothers Animation**

Uncontrolled anger would be another thing from Will Cook's life that we want to throw away and not to keep. A few of Will's children inherited his temper, but none of them (apart from military service) ever killed anyone. Learning to control the tongue is a big part of controlling anger. Thomas Hobbes, speaking of duels, said, " for the most part, they be effects of rash speaking and the fear of dishonour, in one or both the combatants, who, engaged by rashness, are driven into the lists to avoid disgrace."[16] The Good Book puts it succinctly, "He who is slow to anger is better than the mighty, and he who rules his spirit than he who takes a city."[17] Even more succinctly, "Be angry, and sin not."[18]

Righteous anger, though, is an emotion that we should keep. It gives us the courage to confront evil in the world. Sin should make us angry just as the moneychangers made Jesus angry, prompting Him to act in a way that modern society would call "toxic masculinity."

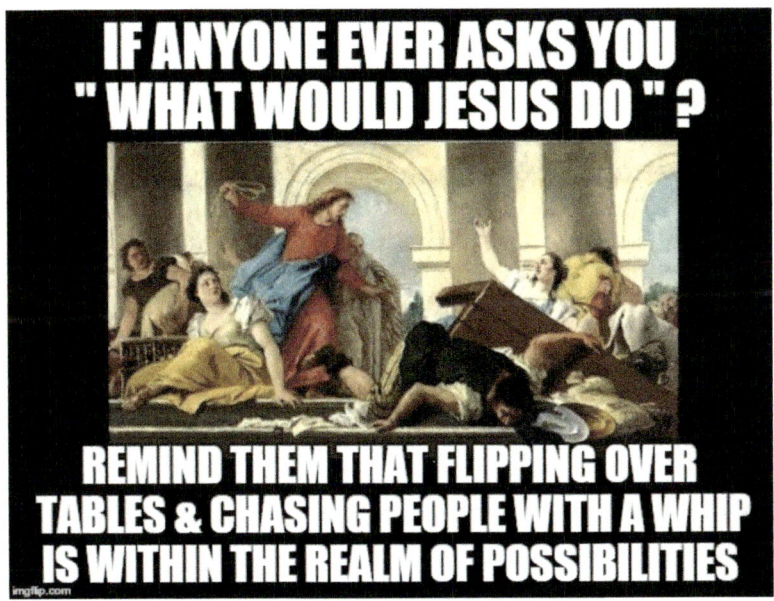

from CentralNYGuy at imgflip.com

John Calvin said, "A dog barks when his master is attacked. I would be a coward if I saw that God's truth is attacked and yet would remain silent."[19] Outrage at evil should make us ready "to fight for the right, without question or pause, to be willing to march into hell for a heavenly cause."[20] "Every time we witness an injustice and do not act, we train our character to be passive in its presence and thereby eventually lose all ability to defend ourselves and those we love."[21]

Chapter Ten

Will Cook was a man of action. He followed the pioneer spirit of men like David Crockett, who said, "Be sure you are right, then go ahead." No one had to tell men of Will's day, "When you're put in charge, take charge." Men like Will had been taking charge since they had gotten out of short britches. They often saw that when you depended on others, you could be disappointed.

Modern society has created men who are scared of almost everything. They are scared of pain. They are scared of crime. They are scared of financial ruin. They are scared of not finding romance. They are scared of storms. They are scared of almost everything except displeasing God. C.S. Lewis said the modern world has created "men without chests," whom "we castrate and then bid the geldings be fruitful."[22] These men have no trust in themselves, no trust in others, no trust in God, and no trust in anything except their own feelings. They will die "unwept, unhonored, and unsung."[23]

Will Cook was not a man who scared easily. If there was a job that had to be done, Will did it, whether it was surviving the Reconstructed South, finding a better life for his family, defending Reelfoot Lake, surviving and cleaning up after floods, surviving and rebuilding after a tornado, defending his daughter's innocence, burying a daughter and a wife, or doing the day-to-day requirements of tenant farming.

Will Cook was a man of honor who took responsibility for the people and things in his stewardship. He was a man who did his duty to his family and to life. Duty and honor teach us, as MacArthur said, "to be proud and unbending in honest failure, but humble and gentle in success; not to substitute words for action; not to seek the path of comfort, but to face the stress and spur of difficulty and challenge; to learn to stand up in the storm, but to have compassion on those who fall;

to master yourself before you seek to master others; to have a heart that is clean, a goal that is high; to learn to laugh, yet never forget how to weep; to reach into the future, yet never neglect the past; to be serious, yet never take yourself too seriously; to be modest so that you will remember the simplicity of true greatness, the open mind of true wisdom, the meekness of true strength."[24]

Modern society needs strong people like Will Cook. "Strong character can rise above the impersonal forces of politics, economics, and even culture to form human destiny and change the flow of history itself."[25]

"Every moment is a window on all time,"[26] as Thomas Wolfe said, and we are connected by blood and by deed to many who have contributed to our existence. If we are wise, we will learn from the mistakes in their lives, but we will also realize the ways in which they excelled us and what we owe to them.

He had flaws, but when one has lived a life of strength, truth, and honor like William Lafayette Cook, even "Nature might stand up and say to all the world, 'This was a man!'"

-THE END-

WORK, FOR THE NIGHT IS COMING

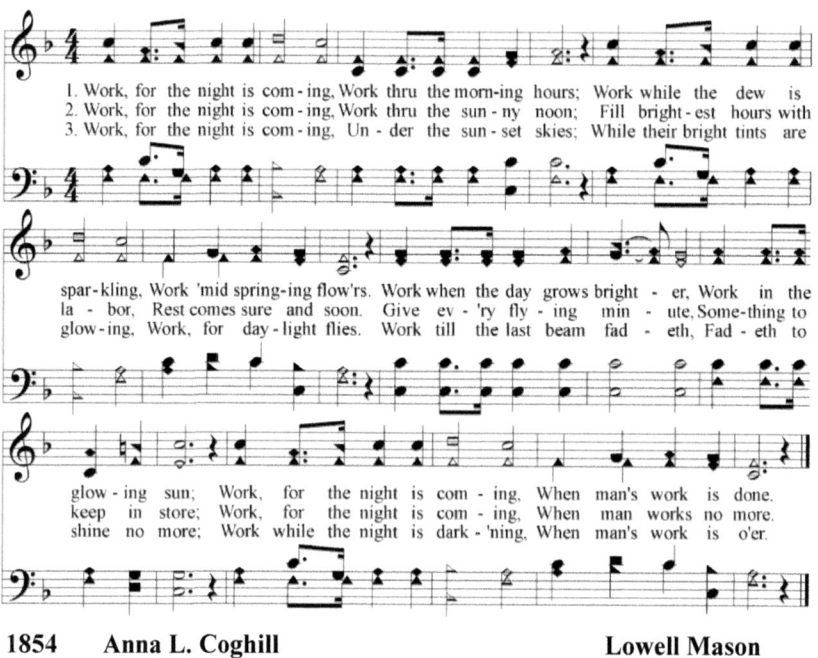

1. Work, for the night is com - ing, Work thru the morn-ing hours; Work while the dew is
2. Work, for the night is com - ing, Work thru the sun - ny noon; Fill bright - est hours with
3. Work, for the night is com - ing, Un - der the sun - set skies; While their bright tints are

spar - kling, Work 'mid spring-ing flow'rs. Work when the day grows bright - er, Work in the
la - bor, Rest comes sure and soon. Give ev - 'ry fly - ing min - ute, Some-thing to
glow - ing, Work, for day - light flies. Work till the last beam fad - eth, Fad - eth to

glow - ing sun; Work, for the night is com - ing, When man's work is done.
keep in store; Work, for the night is com - ing, When man works no more.
shine no more; Work while the night is dark - 'ning, When man's work is o'er.

1854   Anna L. Coghill   **Lowell Mason**

Acknowledgements

This writer sees himself as a compiler rather than an author, and many people have offered a wealth of information worth compiling. I owe a debt of thanks to R E Cook, who embodies many of the qualities that made Will Cook a great man; Pawnee Cook, who shared copies of photographs; Curry Peacock, who gave memories, spiritual insight, and a biscuit pan; Emily Lewis, Loverd Peacock and Paula Henry, who shared memories; Kathleen and Jerry Don Yates, who shared memories and gracious hospitality; Joel and Matt Cook, who shared stories; David Cook, who shared memories; Pat Cook, who gave valuable advice; Alison Cook, who shared her genealogical research; Will Cook's namesakes: William G. Cook of Tennessee, who shared author advice, and William R. Cook of Texas, who proofread; Jane George, who shared memories and accompanied me on fact-finding missions; James and Mike Cook for their memories and proofreading; the late Jackie Boone, for his memories; Tracey Western, who provided memories, proofreading, and a delicious lunch; Kelly Cook for his memories; and Danny Armstrong for wonderful stories and tour services.

In addition, a debt is owed to the late Abigail Rice Hyde, Lake County historian *par excellence*; Dr. Wintfred Smith, who has compiled a monumental trove of Reelfoot Lake material and can seemingly answer any question about Lake County; Arline Orr, Lake County historian and author; George Haynes, native of Lake County, who shook hands with President Truman during his visit and shared memories with me; W.C. Haynes, who shared memories; Shelby Barker, who shared some of his hundreds of stories; J.D. Downing and J.L. "Boochie" Berry, who shared memories; Winston Whitson, who shared photographs, and Albert Markham and Frank T. Markham, long time Lake County residents, who shared memories and whose kinfolk Talmus Markham once employed several Cook siblings.

Valuable assistance was given by the staff of the Tiptonville Library; Karen Elmore of the Paul Meek Library of the University of Tennessee at Martin; Carol Perel, the Executive Director of the

Acknowledgements

West Tennessee Historical Society and an expert on cotton; the staff at the Gordon Browning Museum; the staff of the Tennessee Genealogical Society; the staff at the Tennessee State Library and Archives; the staff of the Kentucky Library Research Collection of Western Kentucky University; the staff of Missouri Historical Society; the staff of Oklahoma Historical Society; all the fine folks who contributed to the Emmett Lewis Museum in Tiptonville; the staff of Reelfoot Lake State Park; the staff of Reelfoot Lake National Wildlife Refuge; author Peggy Scott Holley, who answered some Carroll County questions, and author Jim Emison, who encouraged me to look at difficult stories from the past.

Thanks are also due to John Walker and the Walker family, who provide me a real job while I play at writing on the side; to Dr. Chris Gooch, Nita Gooch, and the rest of the casserole club for their gracious hospitality; to photographers Eleanor Adkison, Dr. Bob Clendenin, Trey Richardson, Debbie Southerland Rogers, and Night Hawk Publishing's John Phillips. Thanks are due to Michael Hendricks of Easton Press, who graciously allowed use of illustrations, and to technical guru Michael Hardrick of TNWEB LLC for domain hosting. I had a wonderful team of proofreaders: Parley Cook, Kristin Beasley, Julie Cook, and Nancy Stewart. Any errors in spelling and grammar are due to the hard-headed - correction - *independently-minded* author, who wouldn't follow the proofreaders' suggestions.

Thanks are also due to all those children of Will Cook who made family reunions of my childhood such a happy time. I didn't realize it at the time, but each reunion of all those aunts and uncles and cousins was, in a way, a celebration of the life of William Lafayette Cook.

Frank Nelson Cook

Chronology

The Life of William Lafayette Cook

October 26, 1874	Will Cook born in Carroll County, Tenn.
1880	Will's mother dies
1885	*Huckleberry Finn* published
1888	Will's brother John moves to Lake County
1895	6.6 earthquake in Charleston, Missouri
1902	Will's brother Joe gets smallpox
	John Cook's 1st wife buried in Carroll Co.
Sept. 20, 1906	Will marries Rachel Hammer in Carroll Co
August 15, 1907	Pauline Cook born in Lauderdale County
1908	Reelfoot Lake Night Riders active
1909	Kathleen Mae Cook born in Carroll County
1910	Halley's Comet appears
c. 1910	Cooks and Richardsons move to Lake Co.
1912	Flooding in Lake County
	Woody Cook and Griffin Cook born
1913	Flooding in Lake County
	John Cook buys land near river
	Malcolm Cook born
1916	L.D. Cook born
1917	America enters the Great War
	Tornado destroys the Cook house
1919	Helen Cook born
	John Cook's son dies of tetanus
	Red scare and race riots in America
1920	Will's wife Rachel becomes a Christian
1921	Will's father Dee dies in Carroll County
	Joe Cook born
	Niece Ludie Richardson dies
1923	Libby Cook born
1926	Baby Cook born and dies

Chronology

1927	Neighbor Zellner Leech is murdered
	Lambert Cook born
	Flooding in Lake County
1929	Great Depression begins
1930	Kathleen Mae Cook dies
1931	Smallpox outbreaks in Lake County
	R E Cook born
	Rachel Emma Hammer Cook dies
1932	Smallpox outbreaks in Lake County
1937	Flooding in Lake County
	John Cook moves to town
1938	Tornado misses Will Cook's house
	John Cook dies
1939	Will Cook moves to town
	Pauline marries on January 21
	First grandchild born on December 2
1941	America enters World War II
1945	President Truman visits Tiptonville
May 24, 1949	Will Cook dies in Lake County, Tenn.

Notes

(see the Bibliography for a complete description of referenced works)

Chapter One

[1] Bragg, *Historic Names and Places of the Lower Mississippi River,* p.43. (Killing an eagle today would incur a $100,000 fine and a year in prison.)

[2] Wallis, *David Crockett,* pp. 7, 169.

[3] Herron, *Things Held Dear*, p. 109.

[4] Cole, *My Hunting Trips to Reelfoot Lake.*

[5] Hayes, *Historic Reelfoot Lake Region*, p.297.

[6] *Public Ledger,* December 30, 1867, February 7, 1871, and November 8, 1882.

[7] *Lexington Herald*, May 21, 1920, p.11.

[8] *Public Ledger,* March 19, 1880, "About Game."

[9] Carter, *Life and Lore of Reelfoot Lake,* p.20.

[10] See the article "Trumpeter Swans," via *www.tnwatchablewildlife.org*, Nashville: Tennessee Wildlife Resources Agency.

[11] Carter, *Life and Lore of Reelfoot Lake*, p.22.

[12] Bishop, *Four Months in a Sneak-box*, pp. 132-133.

[13] *Forest and Stream,* March 30, 1876, "Reel Foot Lake."

[14] *Opelousas Courier,* May 3, 1890, "A Peculiar Lake."

[15] *New York Times,* January 11, 1891, "A Sportsmen's Paradise."

[16] Walker, *Illustrated History of Reelfoot Lake*, p. 23.

[17] Gilchrist, *The Night-Rider's Daughter*, pp.10-11.

[18] Ganier, *Water Birds of Reelfoot Lake, Tennessee.*

[19] Price, "Old Legends Live at Reelfoot Lake," *Southern Living.*

Notes

[20] Eagle, *Reelfoot Lake*, p.92;
Ward, et.al., *Environmental Hydrology*.

[21] *Field and Stream*. Horace V. Wilkins, "A Red-Letter Day on Reelfoot,", December 1927, p. 36.

[22] Humphreys, *The History of the Reelfoot Lake Region*, p.92.

[23] In a letter from Thomas Ferrell to Dr. Alfred M. Franko, Jan.10, 1953; also Abigail Hyde, "Lake County," *Tennessee Encyclopedia of History and Culture*.

[24] "Luster and the Devil," *Why the Possum's Tail is Bare,* p.127.

[25] Smith and Evans, *Archaeological Investigations of the Tiptonville Levee Project*, September 1987.

[26] Three maps produced in 1795 have different names for the same river. The Russel map calls it *Redfoot*. The Tanner map calls it *Reel Foot* (two words). The Carey map calls it *Reelfoot* (one word). Source: Tennessee State Library and Archives.

[27] Eastwood, "The Legend of Reelfoot Lake," May 1910, p.155;
Hickman Courier "Yellow Butterfly Summer," November 25, 1926;
Purcell, *The Birth of Reelfoot Lake and the Legend of Kalopin*, 1929.

[28] Feldman, *When the Mississippi Ran Backwards*, p.9.

[29] *The Stories They Tell*, Lagretta Shaw, p.80.

[30] Caldwell, *Reelfoot Lake*, p. 12.

Chapter Two

[1] Stewart and Knox, *The Earthquake That Never Went Away*, p. 19. There were no seismographs at the time, and scientists differ in their estimates of the magnitude of these quakes, but regardless of the exact numbers, these were massive earthquakes.

[2] Purcell, *Birth of Reelfoot Lake*, p.5.

[3] Carter, *Life and Lore of Reelfoot Lake,* p. 14

[4] Fuller, "The New Madrid Earthquake," p.21.

Notes

[5] Carter, *Life and Lore of Reelfoot Lake*, p.8.

[6] Feldman, *When the Mississippi Ran Backwards*, p.171.

[7] The largest earthquake in U.S. history was one of 9.2 magnitude that struck Anchorage, Alaska in 1964.

[8] Feldman, *When the Mississippi Ran Backwards*, p.236.

[9] The author recalls visiting Tiptonville as a boy and waking up in the night to hear the windows rattling in their frames. No one thought anything of it, and everyone went back to sleep.

[10] Feldman, *When the Mississippi Ran Backwards*, p.238.

[11] *New York Times,* January 11, 1891. "A Sportsmen's Paradise."

[12] Davis, *Lake County Memories,* p.198.

[13] Hyde, "The Beckham Massacre," p.16; Parks, *Like Old Man River*, p. 167; Hayes, *Historic Reelfoot Lake Region*, p.230.

[14] Hayes, *Historic Reelfoot Lake Region*, p.260.

[15] From the "Land Clearing" exhibit at the Reelfoot Lake State Park visitor center.

[16] *Tennessee Republican,* May 23, 1902. The J.N. Cook in this story was Will Cook's brother John. Their other brother Joe Cook visited Lake County, but never moved there.

[17] *Rock Island Argus*, February 3, 1910, p. 5.

[18] Davis, *Lake County Memories,* p. 114, 123.

[19] Fullerton, *A County-wide Screening Program*, p. 78-82.

[20] Davis, *Lake County Memories,* p.187.

[21] Ibid, p. 43, 46, 97.

[22] Ibid, p. 131.

Notes

Chapter Three

[1] Kathleen Yates, in discussion with the author on February 10, 2017, confirmed a conversation the author once overheard between Griffin Cook and Pauline Peacock.

[2] *History of Carroll County, Tennessee*, p.711.

[3] *Carroll County Scrapbook*, April 5, 1877, "How Does the Old Home Look Now?"

[4] Gundersen, "West Tennessee and the Cotton Frontier," p. 25.

[5] See the Carroll County Land Grant book, Gordon Browning Museum and Genealogical Library, McKenzie, Tennessee.

[6] According to the 1850 census, Dee Cook (then age 16), had siblings Louisa A. 25, Harriet S. 22, William A. 20, George M. 18, John H. 14, Martha A. 11, and Mary 6.

[7] Cartmell, *Diaries, Volume II*, October 1860.

[8] Baggett, *The Scalawags*, pp. 85-86, quoting Fielding Hunt of McNairy County.

[9] Holley, *Hawkins' Tories*, p.5.

[10] *Carroll County Democrat*, November 29, 1912.

[11] *History of Carroll County, Tennessee, p.15.*

[12] Baggett, *Homegrown Yankees*, p.68.

[13] Holley, *Hawkins' Tories,* p.38.

[14] The hero of the American Revolution, Marquis de Lafayette, returned to America in 1824-25 in celebration of America's upcoming fiftieth anniversary. He visited and was celebrated in all twenty-four states. Many families named a baby Lafayette at this time, including, no doubt, the McKinney family. William Lafayette Cook was named for his uncle Lafayette McKinney.

[15] In the 1880 census, Will (then age 5), had siblings Mary (Mollie) 14, Nancy 12, Joseph H 10, John N. 8, Francis Amanda 3, and Josie (Ivy) 1.

Notes

[16] Duck, "Memories of Family Life in West Tennessee," p.34.

[17] Will's signature is on his Draft Registration Card, Local Board for Lake County, Tennessee, September 12, 1918.
The 1940 Census of Lake County, Tennessee, tells us Will completed eight grades of schooling..

[18] Draft Registration Card, Local Board for Lake County, Tennessee, September 12, 1918.

[19] Haley, *Roots*, p.645.

[20] John Cook purchased 160 acres in May 1913, 160 acres in Dec. 1913, 155 acres in 1923, 24 acres in 1925, and 140 acres in 1929. Source Lake County, Tennessee, deed books.

[21] *Goodspeed*, p.3

[22] Hyde, *Churches of Lake County.* "Cronanville Cumberland Presbyterian Church."

[23] Wilson, *Life and Ministry of John R. Williams.*

[24] *Milan Exchange*, November 17, 1883, p.5, citing a survey done by the American Bible Society.

[25] According to state records, the first automobiles in Lake County were registered to Judge Harris, R.W. Griffin, and Whit Campbell in May, June, and July of 1906. *Automobile Registrations, Tennessee Secretary of State*, Record Group 111, Box 2, Number 13, Tennessee State Library and Archives.

[26] *Lake County Banner*, "Bessie, A Thriving River Town in 1910," by Norman Parks. April 17, 1969; also Griffin Cook, in discussion with the author, recalled a Brush being the first automobile he ever saw..

[27] Wallis, *David Crockett*, p. 148.

[28] Ibid. p.179.

[29] *Goodspeed*, p.1.

Notes

[30] *Courier Journal*, January 20, 1952, p.109. The newspaper claimed the tree was thirty-nine feet in circumference. In the picture, it doesn't appear to be quite that big. Some sources say thirty-one feet. It was, nevertheless, very large for a cottonwood tree.

[31] Rawls, *Where the Red Fern Grows*, p.89, Chap. IX.

[32] *DuPont Farmers Handbook.*

[33] *History and Families, Lake County*, p.12.

[34] *Hickman Courier*, July 23, 1908, p.1.

[35] *History and Families of Lake County, Tennessee*, p. 136; also, Danny Armstrong, in discussion with the author on September 13, 2014.

[36] Twain, *Life on the Mississippi*, p. 29.

[37] Smith and Evans, *Archeological Investigations of the Tiptonville Levee*, p.19.

[38] *The Stories They Tell, Vol.3*, p.49.

[39] *Lake County Banner,* "Bessie, A Thriving River Town in 1910," by Norman Parks. April 17, 1969.

[40] Parks, *Like Old Man River.* p. 367.

[41] *San Francisco Call* "Flood Victims Feed Animals on House Roofs", Vol. 111, No. 130, April 8, 1912.

[42] Williams, *Mid-South Views the Floods of 1912 and 1913*, p.74.

[43] There were several Dr. Griffins in Lake County. Dr. T. Frank Griffin was a doctor who also served as a member of the Lake County High School Board of Education. He left Lake County after a few years. Dr. R.W. (Dick) Griffin and Dr. Robert (Bob) Griffin both practiced in Lake County for many years; see Lewis, Emmett. "Early Physicians of Madrid Bend and Tiptonville," *Yearbook* of 1996, p.19.

[44] Lowe, *History of Reelfoot Lake*, p.183.

[45] Boone, *Backwoods Woman*, p. 5.

Notes

---

[46]McKenney, *Jack Hinson's One Man War*, p.28.

[47] Nelson, *I Will Hold*, p.7.

Chapter Four

[1] *An act to preserve the public peace,* commonly known as the Ku Klux act, was passed by the 35th Tennessee General Assembly, Extra Session, 1868.

[2] Dickerson, *Haunted Lake*, p. 74.

[3] *Public Ledger*, April 19, 1875, June 1, 1875.

[4] *St. Louis Palladium*, "Happenings in Missouri," July 28, 1906, p. 3.

[5] Vanderwood, *Night Riders of Reelfoot Lake*, p.10.

[6] Hayes, *Historic Reelfoot Lake Region*, p.304.

[7] Albert Markham, in discussion with the author on February 11, 2017.

[8] Vanderwood, *The Night Riders of West Tennessee*, p.54.

[9] This was actually the second time Quentin Rankin had changed sides. He had represented J.C. Harris in the 1902 case *against* the lake supporters before the Tennessee Supreme Court. Then, he had worked *for* the lake supporters to defeat Harris' son in the 1905 case. He won this case by finding a claim to the lake that Harris did not own, one owned by the Galloway heirs of Columbia, Tennessee. He then used that knowledge to go to the heirs and buy their claim so that he could hold the key deed and enrich himself.

[10] Vanderwood in *The Night Riders of West Tennessee,* p.18, says there were 500 families who made their living around the lake. Hayes in *Historic Reelfoot Lake Region*, p.304, says the number was closer to 100.

[11] Vanderwood, *Night Riders of Reelfoot Lake*, p.22.

[12] Ibid, p.30.

[13] Griffin Cook, in discussion with the author.

Notes

[14] Vanderwood, *Night Riders of Reelfoot Lake*, p.25.

[15] Jones, *Lake County Chronicles*, p.8.

[16] Hayes, *Historic Reelfoot Lake Region*, p.314.

[17] Vanderwood, *Night Riders of Reelfoot Lake*, p.44.

[18] Ibid., p. 41, quoting the *Louisville Herald*

[19] Ibid., p.40.

[20] Leonard, *Reelfoot Lake Treasures,* p.17.

[21] Vanderwood, *The Night Riders of West Tennessee*, p. 64.

[22] Vanderwood, *Night Riders of Reelfoot Lake*, p.41.

[23] *Hickman Courier*, October 15, 1908. p.1.

[24] Lowe, *History of Reelfoot Lake*, p. 140.

[25] Humphreys, *The Formation of Reelfoot Lake*, p.63.

Chapter Five

[1] Parks, "Lake County Agriculture, " *The West Tennessee Farm.*

[2] Fullerton, *A County-wide Screening Program,* p.78-82.

[3] Agee, *Cotton Tenants*, p.28.

[4] Fleming, *Civil War and Reconstruction in Alabama.*

[5] Capps, "Memoirs," *Yearbook*, p.7.

[6] Hyde, "Changes in Agriculture," *Hometown Magazine*, p. 30-31.

[7] Capps, "Memoirs," *Yearbook*, p.8.

[8] Hyde, "Changes in Agriculture," *Hometown Magazine*, p. 30-31.

[9] Griffin Cook, in discussion with the author.

Notes

[10] *Lake County Banner*, "From mules to GPS tractors," by John Leeper in an article about Aaron Staulcup, May 3, 2017, p.1.

[11] Frank T. Markham, Jr., in discussion with the author, May 6, 2017.

[12] "Work for the Night is Coming," lyrics by Anna L. Coghill, 1854.

[13] Agee, *Cotton Tenants*, p.129.

[14] Perkins, Tom. *Gems from a Country Gravel Pit*, p.74.

[15] *The Stories They Tell*, Maudie Alford, p. 19.

[16] Grisham, *A Painted House*, Chapter 1, p.10.

[17] The singer Huddie "Leadbelly" Ledbetter popularized the blues song "Pick a Bale of Cotton a Day." Griffin Cook told the author he once picked a bale in a day.

[18] The mechanical cotton picker was invented in 1936, but its use did not become widespread for a long time. The October 10, 1952 *Lake County Banner* had a front page story about new mechanical pickers in the county, but humans did most of the harvesting of cotton for several more decades. Eventually, mechanical pickers put a lot of tenant farmers out of business and caused a great migration of labor to northern factories.

[19] Capps, "Memoirs," *Yearbook*, p.6.

[20] *Lake County Banner*, "Lake County Bygones," by R. C. Donaldson April 11, 1947.

[21] Leaf worms could be killed by calcium arsenate, but unlike the boll weevil, the leaf worm was considered by some farmers to be a helpful insect, because it ate away the leaves and made the cotton bolls easier to see.

[22] *History and Families, Lake County, Tennessee*, p. 19.

[23] The 1925 Tri-States tornado (or tornadoes) killed 747 people. A deadly outbreak in 2011 spawned 362 tornadoes and took 348 lives.

[24] Curry Peacock, in a discussion with the author June 27, 2015.

Notes

[25] We don't know how far Griffin was carried by the tornado. In later years, Griffin claimed it was two miles. The farthest verified distance that a person has been carried by a tornado and lived is 1300 ft, which happened to 19 year old Matt Suter in Missouri in 2006. There is an unverified story of a 22 month old girl named Jewel Butler surviving after being carried ten miles by a 1932 tornado in Alabama. There is another unverified story of a six year old boy named Bennett surviving after being carried ten miles by an 1890 tornado in Villisca, Iowa. These stories come from Grazulis, *Significant Tornadoes*, pp. 133,134, 752

[26] *Memphis Commercial Appeal*, May 28, 1917, p.2. Also, the Tiptonville newspaper reported on March 12, 1926, that Mrs. LeDuke, who had been an invalid since the cyclone, had passed away.

[27] Daniel and Bock, *Island No. 10*, p.120.

[28] *The Stories They Tell*, Harris Freeman Campbell, p.41:
Hickman Courier, May 31, 1917, p.7.

[29] *Hickman Courier*, May 31, 1917, p.17.

[30] *The Stories They Tell*, William Hale Dial, p.56. The communities of Bessie, Cronanville, and Cates Landing were so close that the names were sometimes used interchangeably. Mr. Dial said John Cook's store was in Bessie, but then said it was across from Hopson's store, which was in Cronanville. John Cook's *house* was closer to Bessie. The community of Bessie was about one-half mile south of the Kentucky state line, near the eastern shore of Madrid Bend.

[31] John Cook's obituary stated that he moved to Lake County at age 16 (1888). At age 19 in 1891, he is listed on the voter registration lists for District 1 of Lake County. At age 24, he married Ella Belew of Carroll County, also age 24. Ella died in 1902 and is buried in Furgerson Cemetery in Carroll County. We know that 1902 was also the year that John's brother Joe contracted smallpox while visiting Lake County, so it's possible that John's first wife died of smallpox. John remarried in 1905 to Josie Sorrells of Dyer County.

[32] Carter, *Life and Lore of Reelfoot Lake,* p.65.

[33] John Cook's will, had he survived his wife, would have left the bulk of his estate to either his cousin, or to Lambuth College, a Methodist school in Jackson, Tennessee. After John's wife survived him, the estate passed to her and in turn, she left the bulk of it to her nephew, Roland Campbell, who had been her caregiver. Source: the Will Book, Courthouse, Lake County, Tennessee.

Notes

.

[34] Agee, *Cotton Tenants*, pp, 207-208.

Chapter Six

[1] *Tennessee: A Guide to the State.*

[2] Bordewich, *Bound for Canaan*, p.15

[3] Schlesinger, *The Age of Jackson*, p.424.

[4] Thomas Jefferson, in a letter to John Holmes, written from Monticello, April 22, 1820.

[5] DuPre, *Fagots from the Camp Fire*, Chapter 23, p. 165.

[6] Frank Daniels III editorial, *Nashville Tennessean*, July 19, 2015.

[7] similar to Jose Ortega y Gassett quote, "Create a concept, and reality leaves the room."

[8] Washington, *Up from Slavery*, p. 6.

[9] Foner, *Reconstruction: America's Unfinished Revolution*, p.10, quoting A.L. Taveau, in a letter to the New York Tribune, June 10, 1865.

[10] *Charleston Courier*, April 28, 1862, p.1. When Paris and seven others escaped the Union army, eleven blacks remained behind. These were possibly the same eleven who committed the Beckham massacre in August 1863.

[11] 2 Corinthians 3:17, *Holy Bible*. The most important liberty is the freedom from sin's grip that the spirit of God gives, but as some people studied the Bible, they realized that they should follow God's example and give freedom to the slaves they owned.

[12] Cook, *Buy the Truth and Sell it Not,* p.16.

[13] Baggett, *The Scalawags*, p.102. The planter was David Nunn of Brownsville, Tennessee.

[14] Blount, *Robert E. Lee*, Chapter 5, p. 57.

Notes

[15] Alexander Hamilton, *The Farmer Refuted*, February 5, 1775.

[16] The Federal government had banned the importation of new slaves in 1808, but it did little to enforce the ban. W.E.B. DuBois estimated 250,000 slaves were imported illegally. Other scholars say the figure was closer to 12,000. (Fehrenbacher, *The Slaveholding Republic*, p.149.)

[17] Haley, *Roots*, Chapter 113, p. 643.

[18] Sledge, *With the Old Breed*, p.197.

[19] *History of Carroll County, Tennessee,* p.15. This Mrs. Hawkins was the daughter of R.S. Cole, who earlier gave us descriptions of his Reelfoot Lake hunting trips.

[20] Fleming, *Civil War and Reconstruction in Alabama*, pp. 1-2.

[21] Forrester, Rebel. *Glory and Tears*, Chapter 4.

[22] Cartmell, *Diaries Volume II*, December 1862.

[23] DuBois, *The Souls of Black Folk,* p.17

[24] Fleming, *Civil War and Reconstruction in Alabama,* p.3.

[25] Bacon, *The Negro and the Atlantic Exposition*, p. 6. Miss Bacon's statement is an inversion of von Clausewitz's famous quote that "War is a mere continuation of politics by other means."

[26] DuBois, *The Souls of Black Folks,* p.18.

[27] Washington, *Up from Slavery*, p.40.

[28] Dattel, *Cotton and Race in the Making of America*, p. 281.

[29] Bailey, *Work Among the Colored Brethren*, p. 59. quoting an un-named Baptist leader in 1900.

[30] One example of black superstitions was the belief that you could prevent outsiders from overhearing a conversation by turning a pot upside down in the room. It was believed that this would make a cone of silence that would catch all the sound and keep it from leaving the room. Kannon, *Mighty Rough Times I Tell You,* p.140; *Slave Narratives*, pp.31,45,47,67,77.

Notes

[31] Twain, *Adventures of Huckleberry Finn*, Chap.32, p.167.

[32] Ibid, Chap.23, p.117.

[33] Ibid, Chap. 31, p.161.

[34] Hemingway, *Green Hills of Africa*.

[35] Norman Mailer, *New York Times Review of Books*, December 9, 1984.

[36] Kremer, *George Washington Carver in His Own Words*, p.153.

[37] Lipscomb, *Gospel Advocate*.

[38] *Lake County News*, "Epworth League Program," July 23, 1926, p.1.

[39] Dattel, *Cotton and Race in the Making of America*, p.222.

[40] Ibid., p.346.

[41] Griffin Cook, in discussion with the author.

[42] Vanderwood, *Night Riders of Reelfoot Lake*, p.24.

[43] Danny Armstrong, in discussion with the author September 13, 2014, told the story of Max Richardson and his brothers.

[44] Albert Markham, speaking of his beloved mammy, in discussion with the author February 11, 2017.

[45] Foner, *Reconstruction: America's Unfinished Revolution.* p. 309.

[46] Fehrenbacher, *The Slaveholding Republic*, p.278.

[47] Gibson, *The Negro Holocaust*, Section 3, "Race Riots."

[48] Stockley, *Blood in Their Eyes*, p. 158.

[49] *Tri-County News*, "Tennessee State News," October 12, 1900.

[50] Vandiver, *Lethal Punishment*, p.198.

Notes

[51] Hyde, "1908 Incident at Keefe," *The Night Riders of Reelfoot Lake*, p. 73.

[52] Rolinson, *Grassroots Garveyism*, p.135.

[53] *Commercial*, January 28, 1927, p.1;
Hickman Courier, January 27, 1927, p.1.

[54] The 1993 dystopian novel *The Giver* by Lois Lowry tells of a society in which there is one person who is the keeper of memories for the whole society, so that people don't have to bear the pain of remembering. Unfortunately, modern society today tends toward this practice by either forgetting history, or rewriting it to suit current beliefs.

[55] Woody Cook, in discussion with the author on June 26, 2004 at the family reunion in Tiptonville, Tennessee.

[56] Some examples of blacks who died in northern Lake County are: Ed Moffit, a 35 year old black, shot to death in November 1926; Nathaniel Jones, a 16 year old black, shot by shotgun in December 1926; James Ellis, a 36 year old black, death from gunshot wounds in December 1926, Wesley Roberson, a 45 year old black, died of heart failure in November 1924, Hart Smith, a 24 year old black, death by paralysis, no physician in March 1929, Henry Hunt, a 31 year old black, died of apolplexy in June 1925, Lincoln Stewart, a 70 year old black, of unknown cause in December 1925, and Rosevelt Johnson, a 19 year old black, of T.B. in August 1926.

[57] A somewhat similar story has been told by R E Cook, Curry Peacock, Matt Cook, Joel Cook, and Shelby Barker, all in discussion with the author. If we pick an arbitrary date of 1925, Will's daughters would have been age 18 (Pauline), 16 (Kathleen), 6 (Helen), and 2 (Libby).

[58] Will had a violent temper, according to Kathleen Yates, in discussion with the author February 14, 2015. According to Kathleen, her father once shielded a sibling from a violent whipping by Will.

[59] Nixon, "Whither Southern Economy," *I'll Take My Stand*, p.176, quoting Sidney Lanier.

Chapter Seven
[1] McKay, *Honor in the American South* and *How to be an Honorable Man*.

Notes

[2] William Shakespeare, *The Tragedy of Hamlet, Prince of Denmark*, Act I, Scene iii, written about 1600.

[3] Emerson, *Voluntaries*, 1863.

[4] Doyle, *The Private of the Buffs*.

[5] William Shakespeare, *King Henry V*, Act IV, Scene iii, written about 1599.

[6] Hebrews 2:7. *Holy Bible*

[7] Ancient Spartan warriors often used long shields that would shield the whole body. If they died in battle, the shield could be used to carry the body home. If an army was running away from the enemy, they would discard their shields along with their honor so they could run faster. Hence, "Come home with your shield, or on it."

[8] General William Giles Harding letter to J. George Harris, Belle Meade, Tennessee, February 9, 1877. *Historic Magazine and Notes and Queries*, p.205.

[9] Vandiver, *Lethal Punishment,* p.30.quoting William Lynnwood Montell.

[10] Twain, *Life on the Mississippi*, p.157; Some of the Lake County feuds were Darnell-Watson, Everett-Moore, Darnell-Lane, and Nall-Darnell; according to Harris, "Personal Recollections" *2002 Yearbook*, p.26.

[11] Hayes, *Historic Reelfoot Lake Region*, p.270.

[12] *Hickman Courier*, May 28, 1925, p.1.

[13] *Hickman Courier*, March 21, 1929. *Indianapolis Star*, March 18, 1929, p.32.

[14] Vandiver, *Lethal Punishment*, p. 89, quoting Charles J. Bonaparte.

[15] Wyatt-Brown, *Southern Honor*, p.43.

[16] Ibid., p.53.

[17] J.M. Rushing of the Mercer (Georgia) Baptist Association, "Lynch Law or no Lynch Law," *Nashville Banner*, October 22, 1908, p.2.

[18] Frank T. Markham, Jr., in discussion with the author, May 6, 2017.

Notes

---

[19] The Icelandic language also has several words for snow.

[20] Cicero, *De Officiis*, I. vii. (23). When the printing press was invented, Cicero's book was the second one ever printed, right after the Bible.

[21] Exodus 21:12-13, *Holy Bible*. God provided cities of refuge where those accused of manslaughter could flee.

[22] Ezekiel 18:20, Deuteronomy 24:16, *Holy Bible*.

[23] Exodus 20:6, *Holy Bible*, part of the Ten Commandments.

[24] Lamentations 5:7, *Holy Bible*.

Chapter Eight

[1] *Lake County, Tennessee Rural Electrification* map of 1935, Tennessee State Library and Archives.

[2] James 4:14. *Holy Bible*.

[3] Parks, *Like Old Man River,* p.338.

[4] Griffin Cook, in discussion with the author.

[5] *Lake County News*, June 20, 1924. Reprinted in *Lake County Historical Society 2003 Yearbook,* p.8.

[6] Griffin Cook in discussion with the author, sometimes used that saying. He told the author that he had swum the Mississippi to the Missouri shore and back.

[7] Lee, *To Kill A Mockingbird*, Chap. 1.

[8] Parks, *Like Old Man River,* p.15.

[9] Wilson, *Life and Ministry of John R, Williams,* p.5.

[10] Parks, *Like Old Man River,* p.433.

[11] Ibid,, p. 433.

Notes

[12] Davis, *Lake County Memories,* p. 121. Mrs. Will Cook's obituary of Nov. 20, 1931.

[13] Perkins, Laverne. "Jones Chapel Church of Christ," *Churches of Lake County, Tennessee.* The original building burned and was replaced by the current structure.

[14] Wilson, *Life and Ministry of John R. Williams,* p.20.

[15] Parks, *Like Old Man River,* p. 434.

[16] Kathleen Yates, in discussion with the author February 14, 2015.

[17] *Cook Book*, p.16.

[18] Parks, *Like Old Man River,* p. 337.

[19] Acts 9:5. *Holy Bible.*

[20] Eagle, *Reelfoot Lake Fishing and Duck Shooting,*. p. 37.

[21] Henson, *Just Plain Brady*, p. 48.

[22] Vanderwood, *Night Riders of Reelfoot Lake*, p. 9.

[23] Waylon Jennings, *Good Ole Boys*, theme song of television show *The Dukes of Hazzard*, 1979.

[24] Griffin Cook, "A Sports Thrill."

[25] Carter, *Life and Lore of Reelfoot Lake,* p.70.

[26] *The Stories They Tell*, Iona Chamberlain, p.51.

[27] Davis, *Lake County Memories,* p.22.

[28] Ibid, p.12.

[29] Loverd Peacock's football instincts once kicked in during a basketball game shortly after football season had ended.

[30] Davis, *Lake County Memories,* p.24, 46.

Notes

[31] Parks, *Like Old Man River,* p. 455.

[32] Hayes, *Historic Reelfoot Lake Region*, p.196.

[33] *Lake County Banner*, October 31, 1930, p.1. Also, Davis, *Lake County Memories*, p. 112.

[34] Dyer County Court records, Tennessee State Library and Archives. Coincidentally, there was a judge on the Tennessee Supreme Court who was also named William L. Cook. He seems to be no relation, and the name didn't help bring justice for Will Cook's daughter.

[35] One baby had been born dead on April 6, 1926 and was buried in a nearby cemetery.

[36] Jane George, in discussion with the author concerning what Griffin Cook had told her.

[37] Jim Cook and Mike Cook, in discussion with the author, March 18, 2016.

[38] Griffin Cook

Chapter Nine

[1] Abigail Hyde, in discussion with the author, February 13, 2015.

[2] Parks, *Like Old Man River,* p. 467.

[3] 2 Thessalonians 3:10, *Holy Bible*.

[4] *The Stories They Tell*, Alpharetta Turner Bargery, p.28.

[5] Griffin Cook, in discussion with the author.

[6] Kathleen Yates, in discussion with the author February 14,2015.

[7] Parks, *Like Old Man River*, p.469.

[8] *Lake County Banner*, March 15, 1938.

[9] *Lake County Banner*, May 27, 1938.

[10] *Lake County News*, July 9, 1926, p. 1, as one example.

Notes

[11] Hiram Sylvester "Syl" Sutton was also a native of Carroll County, having been born there in 1870. He died in 1964 in Tiptonville, with services held at the Tiptonville Church of Christ. He was a friend of Will Cook, according to R E Cook, in discussion with the author October 15, 2015.

[12] Davis, *Lake County Memories*, p.200. Will attended the Reelfoot FFA father-son banquet on April 7, 1938.

[13] Mary Cook, as told by her daughter Tracey, in discussion with the author, June 25, 2016.

[14] Curry Peacock, in discussion with the author June 25, 2016.

[15] David Cook, in discussion with the author.

[16] R E Cook, in discussion with the author June 27, 2015.

[17] Griffin's wife Claire, in discussion with the author. She was a teacher at Tiptonville High School in the 1938-39 school year. Her contract perhaps was not renewed because of her religious affiliation. In the early 1930s, Norman Parks said that no Church of Christ member had ever been employed in the school system: *Like Old Man River,* p. 464.

[18] Kathleen Yates, in discussion with the author February 10, 2017.

[19] William Cullen Bryant, *Thanatopsis*. 1817.

[20] R E Cook and Curry Peacock, in discussion with the author, June 25, 2016.

[21] Will was survived by daughters, Mrs. Pauline Peacock of Tiptonville, Miss Helen Cook of Memphis, Mrs. J.H. Boone of Milan; by sons, Woodrow Cook of Tiptonville, Griffin Cook of Lewisburg, Tenn., Malcolm Cook with the U.S. Marines in Norfolk, Virginia, L.D. Cook of Tiptonville, Joe Cook of Memphis, Lambert Cook of Searcy, Ark., R E Cook of Tiptonville; and by sisters, Mrs. Will Dargell of New Orleans and Mrs. Mollie Matthews of Gillett, Ark. *Dyersburg State Gazette*, May 25, 1949.

Chapter Ten

[1] Line suggested by the song, *The Gambler*, lyrics by Don Schlitz, August, 1976.

[2] Job 27: 1-5, *Holy Bible*

Notes

[3] A picture taken at Highlander Folk School in Monteagle, Tennessee shows Abner Berry of the Central Committee of the Communist Party USA, Communists Myles Horton and Aubrey Williams seated alongside Dr. Martin Luther King. Communists wanted to use civil rights leaders to promote their own godless causes. They tried to recruit Dr. King to be their agent, but he was too committed to the principles of American democracy and freedom to join them. Their influence, however, may have led him to join the anti-war movement and the supporting of illegal labor strikes, such as in Memphis, where he was killed.

[4] Blount, *Crackers,* p.278.

[5] Genesis 11:1-9. *Holy Bible.*

[6] Genesis 1:27, 3:20. *Holy Bible.*

[7] Ecclesiastes 1:9. *Holy Bible.*

[8] Proverbs 22:28. *Holy Bible.*

[9] Jeremiah 6:16. *Holy Bible.*

[10] The Tennessee Children's Home Society in Memphis (NOT to be confused with the Tennessee Children's Home in Spring Hill) did some terrible crimes, such as telling mothers that their babies had died, so that they could then sell the baby to someone else, but they never murdered babies, which is an abortion clinic's stock in trade.

[11] Kipling, *The Gods of The Copybook Headings*. The geological layer of rock that was rhen called *Feminian* is today referred to as *Permian*.

[12] Lewis, C.S. *Letters of C.S. Lewis*, p.447.

[13] This is the author's parody of Rudyard Kipling's "The Law of the Wolves" from *The Second Jungle Book*, chapter two. Kipling's verse is as follows: "Now this is the law of the jungle, as old and as true as the sky. And the wolf that shall keep it may prosper, but the wolf that shall break it must die. As the creeper that girdles the tree trunk, the law runneth forward and back; for the strength of the pack is the wolf, and the strength of the wolf is the pack."

[14] Robert A. Heinlein, speech to the U.S. Naval Academy at Annapolis, April 5, 1973.

Notes

[15] A man shall leave father and mother and be joined to his wife, and they shall become one flesh (Genesis 2:24, *Holy Bible*); He who made them at the beginning made them male and female ... what God has joined together, let not man separate. (Matthew 19:4-6, *Holy Bible*)

[16] Hobbes, "Of Power, Worth, Dignity, Honor, and Worthiness," Chapter Ten, *Of Man*, being the first part of *Leviathan.*

[17] Proverbs 16:32. *Holy Bible.*

[18] Psalm 4:4, Ephesians 4:26. *Holy Bible.*

[19] John Calvin to the queen of Navarre (a kingdom between France and Spain), April 28, 1545.

[20] lyrics by Joe Darrion, "The Impossible Dream," *Man of La Mancha,* a 1964 Broadway musical.

[21] Julian Assange, Victoria, Australia: via www.iq.org, January 3, 2007.

[22] Lewis, C.S. *The Abolition of Man*, chapter 1, p.26.

[23] Sir Walter Scott, *The Lay of the Last Minstrel*, Canto VI. This expression by Scott is similar to Achilles' description in Pope's translation of the *Illiad*, that Hector was "unwept, unhonor'd, uninterred."

[24] General Douglas MacArthur, *Duty, Honor, Country*, speech to the Corps of Cadets at the U.S. Military Academy at West Point, New York, May 12, 1962.

[25] Joseph Epstein, *The Art of Biography*, speech at Hillsdale College Center for Constructive Alternatives III, January 31, 2016.

[26] Wolfe. *Look Homeward, Angel.* p.5.
William Shakespeare, *The Tragedy of Julius Caesar, Act V, Scene V*. 1599.

Notes

Wall map, Emmett Lewis Museum in Tiptonville

Glossary of Terms and Expressions

Bayou de Chein. Pronounced "Bay de Shay" or "By de Shay," French for "Creek of the Dog." One of Reelfoot Lake's tributaries, named by French trappers for the many Indian dogs they observed.

buoy. Pronounced "boy." A floating platform anchored to the river bottom to mark the edge of the main river channel.

busy as a cranberry merchant at Christmastime. Very busy.

can to can't. Working from the early dawn, when one first can see, until the last twilight of the evening fades, when one can't see.

chimney-corner scripture. Wise sayings that sound like scripture, but are not in the Bible.

ciphering. Doing arithmetic.

copacetic. Completely satisfactory.

couldn't hit the broad side of a barn. Used to describe someone who is a poor shot with a firearm or any projectile.

dead as a doornail. With no life whatsoever.

fat as a town dog. Well-fed, the way a kept animal becomes, as opposed to a lean one that hunts its own food in the country.

first pop out of the book. On the first try or at the first opportunity, often unexpectedly.

gee-haw. Often used in the negative to describe someone who doesn't cooperate well with another, a reference to the commands given to a mule to turn right (*gee*) or left (*haw*).

Good Book. the Holy Bible.

Glossary of Terms and Expressions

go to bed with the chickens. Go to sleep soon after dark.

gotten out of short britches. Grew from being a little boy to an older boy with chores and responsibilities.

handy as a pocket on a shirt. Very useful.

highfalutin. Pompous or pretentious.

it don't matter how thin you cut the baloney, it's still got two sides. There are two sides to every story.

independent as a hog on ice. An unpredictable, self-directed individual.

iota. A tiny amount

lead poisoning. Death caused by bullets.

like a chicken with his head cut off. Much action with little accomplishment.

like a duck on a June bug. With promptness and enthusiasm.

lit out like a scalded dog. Moved quickly away from something.

lo and behold, An exclamation of surprise calling attention to something unexpected.

many a slip 'twixt the cup and the lip. A failure to deliver what was promised, whether from an unsteady cup or an unsteady person.

more than Carter had oats. An abundance, originally referring to a Georgia plantation owner who had a bumper crop of oats.

Glossary of Terms and Expressions

no step for a stepper. Sometimes rendered in other places as **no hill for a stepper,** but Lake County has no hills. Either phrase refers to a task that is not a problem for someone who is determined to do it.

playing possum. Pretending to be dead, or to be asleep.

plus ça change. Pronounced (approximately) "Plew sa Shawnz."A short form of the French epigram by Jean-Baptiste Alphonse Karr, *plus ça change, plus c'est la meme chose,* meaning the more things change, the more they remain the same. (a companion thought to Emerson's remark that "society never advances")

rabbits' dance. A social interaction of wild rabbits in which they gather in a circle at night and individually dance in complete silence.

slough. Pronounced "slew." A channel which, during times of flooding, carries water as a river or stream, but at other times is a body of standing water.

struck by lightning on a clear night. Destroyed by arson.

susie. A female duck.

tough as Dubble-Bubble®. A reputation for being hard and tough, like the bubblegum of that name.

Uncle / Aunt. A title of endearment once used of black friends, especially older ones, e.g. "Uncle Remus." The terms are now viewed as racist or patronizing.

walking in high cotton. Reaping a bountiful crop.

wouldn't hit a lick at a snake. Lazy.

wouldn't work in a pie factory. Very lazy.

Plowing in New Madrid, Missouri

Bibliography

Agee, James. *Cotton Tenants*. Brooklyn: Melville House, 2013.

Bacon, Alice M. *The Negro and the Atlantic Exposition*. Baltimore: Trustees of the John F.Slater Fund Occasional Papers, No. 7; 1896.

Baggett, James Alex. *The Scalawags*. Baton Rouge: Louisiana State University Press, 2003.

Baggett, James Alex. *Homegrown Yankees: Tennessee's Union Cavalry in the Civil War*. Baton Rouge: Louisiana State University Press, 2009.

Bailey, Fred Arthur. *Work Among the Colored Brethren*. Memphis: West Tennessee Historical Society, Vol. 55, 2001.

Bishop, Nathaniel Holmes. *Four Months in a Sneak-box: A Boat Voyage of 2600 Miles Down the Ohio and Mississippi Rivers*. Bedford, Mass: Applewood Books, 1879.

Blount, Roy, Jr. *Crackers*. Athens, Georgia: Universiy of Georgia Press, 1977.

Blount, Roy, Jr. *Robert E. Lee*. New York: Viking Press, 2003.

Boone, Jack. *Backwoods Woman*. New York: J.B. Lippincott, 1939.

Bordewich, Fergus M. *Bound for Canaan*. New York: HarperCollins, 2005.

Bragg, Marvin. *Historic Names and Places on the Lower Mississippi River*. Vicksburg, Miss: Mississippi River Commission, 1977..

Caldwell, Russell H., *Reelfoot Lake: History – Duck Call Makers – Hunting Tales*. Union City, Tenn: Caldwell's Office Outfitters, 1988.

Capps, Elvis. "Memoirs." *Yearbook*. Tiptonville: Lake County Historical Society, 1997.

Carroll County Democrat. Huntingdon, Tennessee.

Carroll County Scrapbook. Mollie Grizzard, editor. Nashville: Tennessee State Library and Archives, Microfilm 251.

Carter, John Ray. *Life and Lore of Reelfoot Lake*. Nashville: George Peabody College for Teachers, Masters Thesis, August 1958.

Cartmell, Robert H. *Diaries, Volume II*. Nashville: Tennessee State Library and Archives unpublished manuscript, 1860 – 1862.

Charleston Courier. Charleston, South Carolina.

Cicero, Marcus Tullius. *De Officiis*, 44 B.C.

Bibliography

Clay, Floyd M, Ph.D. *A Century on the Mississippi*. Memphis: U.S. Army Corps of Engineers, 1986.

Clendenin, Robert E., Jr. *Reelfoot Lake Images*. Union City, Tenn: Lanzer Printing, 2009.

Cobb, Irvin S. *Fishhead*, a short story. 1913.

Cole, Richmond Swinney (1807-1902). *My Hunting Trips to Reelfoot Lake*. University of Tennessee at Martin, Paul Meek Library: unpublished manuscript in the Wintfred Smith Special Collection, 1891. (R.S. Cole moved to Carroll County in 1832, and his trips to Reelfoot began shortly thereafter.)

The Commercial. Union City, Tenn.

Cook Book. Union City, Tenn: Ladies Aid Society of the First Christian Church, 1916; reprinted by Lanzer Printing, Union City, 1975.

Cook, Frank N. *Buy the Truth and Sell it Not: The Life of E. Gaston Collins*. Lewisburg, Tenn: Unclouded Press, 2014.

Cook, Griffin. "A Sports Thrill." *The Nashville Tennessean Magazine*. October 23, 1949.

Courier Journal. Louisville, Kentucky.

Crockett, David. *A Narrative of the Life of David Crockett of the State of Tennessee*. Lincoln, Neb: University of Nebraska Press, 1987. Originally published Philadelphia: Carey and Hart, 1834.

Daniel, Larry J., and Lynn N. Bock. *Island No. 10: Struggle for the Mississippi Valley*. Tuscaloosa: University of Alabama Press, 1996.

Dattel, Gene. *Cotton and Race in the Making of America*. Chicago: Ivan R. Dee, 2009.

Davis, Dr. Emily. *Lake County Memories: History in Newsprint and Pictures*. Humboldt, Tenn: Rose Publishing, 1998.

Devens, R.M. *Our First Century*. Springfield, Mass.: C.A. Nichols, 1877.

Dickerson, Harris. "Haunted Lake." *Colliers* magazine. New York: May 29, 1937.

Doyle, Sir Francis. "The Private of the Buffs." *The English Poets, Vol. V*, edited by Thomas Humphrey Ward. New York: MacMillian, 1918.

Bibliography

DuBois, W.E.B. *The Souls of Black Folk*. New York: Dover, 1994. originally published in Chicago: A.C. McClurg, 1903.

Duck, Edward Walker. *Memories of Family Life in West Tennessee from Around 1890 to 1910*. Memphis: West Tennessee Historical Society, Vol. 25, 1971.

DuPont Farmers Handbook. Wilmington, Delaware: E.I. DuPont deNemours, 1912.

DuPre, L.J. *Fagots from the Camp Fire*. New York: Emily Thornton Charles & Co., 1881.

Eagle, R.E. Lee. *Reelfoot Lake Fishing and Duck Shooting*. Nashville: McQuiddy Printing, 1915.

Eastwood, Vera. "The Legend of Reelfoot Lake." *The Taylor-Trotwood Magazine* Vol. XI, No.1. Nashville: The Taylor Publishing Co., May, 1910.

Emerson, Ralph Waldo. "Voluntaries." *Works of Ralph Waldo Emerson*. Boston: Houghton, Mifflin, and Sons, 1876.

Fehrenbacher, Don E. *The Slaveholding Republic*. New York: Oxford University Press, 2001.

Feldman, Jay. *When the Mississippi Ran Backwards*. New York: Free Press, 2005.

Field and Stream magazine. New York.

Fleming, Walter L. *Civil War and Reconstruction in Alabama*. New York: Columbia University Press, 1905.

Foner, Eric. *Reconstruction: America's Unfinished Revolution*. New York: Harper and Row, 1988.

Forest and Stream magazine, Charles Halleck, editor. New York.

Forrester, R.C. and Betty Burdick Wood. *Night Riders of Reelfoot Lake: The Untold Story*. Union City, Tenn: Forrester/Wood, 2001.

Forrester, Rebel C. *Glory and Tears*. Union City, Tenn: H.A. Lanzer Co., 1970.

Fuller, Myron L. *The New Madrid Earthquake* Bulletin #494. Washington, D.C.: U.S. Geological Survey, 1912.

Fullerton, Howard A. *A County-wide Screening Program*. Nashville: Journal of Tenn. Academy of Science 4(3), 1929.

Bibliography

Ganier, Albert F. *Water Birds of Reelfoot Lake, Tennessee.*
Nashville: Journal of Tenn. Academy of Science, 1933.

Gibson, Robert A. *The Negro Holocaust: Lynching and Race Riots in the United States 1880-1950.* Connecticut: Yale-New Haven Teachers Institute, 1979.

Gilchrist, Annie Somers. *The Night-Rider's Daughter.* Nashville: Marshall & Bruce Co., 1910.

Goodspeed History of Tennessee, History of Lake County. Nashville: Goodspeed Publishing, 1887.

Grazulis, Thomas P. *Significant Tornadoes.* St Johnsbury, Vermont: Environmental Films, July 1993.

Grisham, John. *A Painted House.* New York: Doubleday, 2000.

Gundersen, Lawrence G., Jr. "West Tennessee and the Cotton Frontier 1818-1840." Memphis: West Tennessee Historical Society, Vol. 52, 1998.

Haley, Alex. *Roots.* Garden City, New York: Doubleday, 1976.

Harris, James C. "Personal Recollections of this County – February 1900." *Yearbook.* Tiptonville: Lake County Historical Society, 2002.

Hayes, David G. *The Historic Reelfoot Lake Region.* Collierville, Tenn: InstantPublisher, 2017.

Hemingway, Ernest. *Green Hills of Africa.* New York: Charles Scribner's Sons, 1935.

Henson, Rick. *Just Plain Brady.* Baltimore: PublishAmerica, 2004.

Herron, Roy. *Things Held Dear.* Louisville: Westminster John Knox Press, 1999.

Hickman Courier. Hickman, Kentucky.

Historic Magazine and Notes and Queries, N.B. Webster, editor. Manchester, New Hampshire: S.C. Gould, publisher.

History of Carroll County, Tennessee. Paducah, Kentucky: Turner Publishing, 1986.

History and Families of Lake County, Tennessee, edited by Hubert Perkins. Paducah, Kentucky: Turner Publishing, 1992.

Hobbes, Thomas. "Of Power, Worth, Dignity, Honor, and Worthiness." *Of Man* being the first part of *Leviathan.* Oxford: Clarendon Press, 1651.

Bibliography

Holley, Peggy Scott. *Hawkins' Tories*. Dickson, Tenn: BrayBree Publishing, 2014.

Humphreys, Cecil C. *The History of the Reelfoot Lake Region*. Knoxville: University of Tennessee Masters Thesis, August 1938.

Humphreys, Cecil C. *The Formation of Reelfoot Lake and Consequent Land and Social Problems*. Memphis: West Tennessee Historical Society, 1960.

Hyde, Abigail. "Cronanville Cumberland Presbyterian Church." *Churches of Lake County, Tennessee*. Tiptonville, Tenn: Lake County Historical Society, 1981.

Hyde, Abigail. "Changes in Agriculture." *Hometown Magazine*. South Fulton, Tenn: April, 2000.

Hyde, Abigail. "1908 Incident at Keefe." *The Night Riders of Reelfoot Lake*. Tiptonville, Tenn: Lake County Historical Society, 2000.

Hyde, Abigail. "The Beckham Massacre." *Yearbook*. Tiptonville, Tenn: Lake County Historical Society, 2004.

Hyde, Abigail. "Lake County." via online *Tennessee Encyclopedia of History and Culture*. Knoxville, Tenn: University of Tennessee Press.

Indianapolis Star. Indianapolis, Indiana.

Johnson, Clifton. *Highways and Byways of the Mississippi Valley*. New York: Macmillian, 1906.

Jones, Evan. *Lake County Chronicles*. Tiptonville, Tenn: Lake County Banner, 2012.

Kannon, Ellis Ken. "They Would Turn a Kettle Upside Down." *Might Rough Times, I Tell You*, edited by Andrea Sutcliffe. Winston-Salem, North Carolina: John F. Blair, Publisher, 2000.

Kipling, Rudyard. "The Gods of the Copybook Headings." *Stories and Poems*. Oxford University Press, 1999.

Kremer, Gary R. *George Washington Carver in His Own Words*. Columbia, Missouri: University of Missouri Press, 1987.

Lake County Banner. Tiptonville, Tenn.

Lake County News. Tiptonville, Tenn.

Bibliography

L'amour, Louis. *The Walking Drum*. New York: Bantam Books, 1984.

Lee, Harper. *To Kill a Mockingbird*. New York: Grand Central Publishing, 1960.

Leonard, Lexie. *Reelfoot Lake Treasures*. Tiptonville, Tenn: Lake County Banner, 1991.

Lewis, C.S. *The Abolition of Man*. Oxford University Press, 1943.

Lewis, C.S. "Letter to Mrs. Ashton of March 16, 1955." *Letters of C.S. Lewis*, edited by Warren Lewis. Orlando: Harcourt, 1988.

Lewis, Emmett. "Early Physicians of Madrid Bend and Tiptonville." *Yearbook*. Tiptonville: Lake County Historical Society, 1996.

Lexington Herald. Lexington, Kentucky.

Lipscomb, David. "The Negro – his crimes and treatment." *Gospel Advocate* #43, p.600. Nashville, Tenn. September 19, 1901.

Longfellow, Henry Wadsworth. "A Psalm of Life." *The Complete Poetic Works of Longfellow*. Boston: Houghton Mifflin Company, 1893.

Lowe, Walter Edgar. *History of Reelfoot Lake*. Nashville: George Peabody College for Teachers Masters Thesis, August 1930.

"Luster and the Devil." *Why the Possum's Tail is Bare*, edited by Jimmy Neil Smith. New York: Avon Books, 1993.

Maslowski, Karl H. and W.W. Goodpaster, *Earthquake Lake*, video recording in the Paul Meek Library, Univ. of Tenn. at Martin.

McKay, Brent and Kate, *Honor in the American South* and *How to be an Honorable Man*. Jenks, Oklahoma: weblog via www.artofmanliness.com, 2012.

McKenney, Tom C. *Jack Hinson's One Man War*. Gretna, Louisiana: Pelican Publishing, 2009.

Medved, Michael and Diane. *Saving Childhood: Protecting Our Children from the National Assault on Innocence*. New York: HarperCollins, 1998.

Memphis Commercial Appeal. Memphis, Tenn.

Milan Exchange. Milan, Tenn.

Nashville Banner. Nashville, Tenn.

Nashville Tennessean. Nashville, Tenn.

Bibliography

Nelson, James Carl. *I Will Hold: The story of USMC legend Clifton B. Cates, from Belleau Wood to victory in the Great War*. New York: Caliber press, 2016.

New York Times. New York, NY.

Nixon, Herman Clarence. "Whither Southern Economy?" *I'll Take My Stand*. Baton Rouge: Louisiana State University Press, 2006.

Opelousas Courier. Opelousas, Louisiana.

Parks, Norman L. "Lake County Agriculture." *The West Tennessee Farm*, edited by Marvin Downing. University of Tennessee at Martin, 1979.

Parks, Norman L. *Like Old Man River: A History of the Parks, Crafton, Boshears, McGuire, Tipton, and Dial families from 1607-1986*. Murfreesboro, Tenn: self-published, 1986.

Patton, James Welch. *Unionism and Reconstruction in Tennessee*. Chapel Hill, N.C.: University of North Carolina Press, 1934.

Perkins, Laverne Huffstutter. "Jones Chapel Church of Christ." *Churches of Lake County, Tennessee*. Tiptonville, Tenn: Lake County Historical Society, 1981.

Perkins, Tom. *Gems from a Country Gravel Pit*. Jackson, Tenn: Main Street Publishing, 2014.

Price, Steve. "Old Legends Live at Reelfoot Lake." *Southern Living*. March, 1977.

Public Ledger. Memphis, Tenn.

Purcell, Martha Grassham. *Birth of Reelfoot Lake and the Legend of Kalopin*. Paducah, Kentucky: Paducah Printing, 1929.

Rawls, Wilson. *Where the Red Fern Grows*. NewYork: Random House, 1961.

Rolinson, Mary G. *Grassroots Garveyism*. Chapel Hill: University of North Carolina Press, 2007.

Rock Island Argus. Rock Island, Illinois.

Sabin Photograph Collection. Donald V. Sabin. Tennessee State Library and Archives. Microfilm #1503, Accession #MSS89-115.

San Francisco Call. San Francisco, California.

Schlesinger, Arthur M., Jr. *The Age of Jackson*. Boston: Little, Brown and Company, 1945.

Bibliography

Shaffer, James L. and John T. Tigges. *The Mississippi River: Father of Waters*. Charleston, S.C.: Arcadia Publishing, 2000.

Slave Narratives: Measy Hudson, Ann Matthews, John Moore, Millie Simpkins, Sylvia Watkins. Washington, D.C.: Federal Writers Project, 1941.

Sledge, E.B., *With the Old Breed*, Novato, Calif: Presidio Press, 1981.

Smith, Gerald P. and E. Raymond Evans. *Archeological Investigations of the Tiptonville Levee Project*. Memphis: Dept. of the Army Corps of Engineers, 1987.

St. Louis Palladium. St. Louis, Missouri.

Stewart, Dr. David and Dr. Ray Knox. *The Earthquake That Never Went Away*. Marble Hill, Missouri: Gutenberg-Richter Publications, 1993.

Stockley, Grif. *Blood in Their Eyes*. Fayetteville, Ark: University of Arkansas Press, 2001.

Stowe, Harriet Beecher. *Uncle Tom's Cabin: A Tale of Life Among the Lowly*. London: George Routledge & Co., 1852.

Summers, Judy and Ivey. *Night Riders of Reelfoot Lake Scrapbook*. Walnut Log, Tenn: self-published, 1996.

Tennessee: A Guide to the State. Federal Writers Project. Nashville: Tennessee Dept. of Conservation, December 1939.

Tennessee Republican. Huntingdon, Tennessee.

The Stories They Tell. Maudie Alford, Alpharetta Turner Bargery, Harris Freeman Campbell, Iona Chamberlain, William Hale Dial, Lagretta Shaw. Tiptonville, Tenn: Lake County Historical Society, 1988.

*The Stories They Tell, Vol.*3, Tiptonville, Tenn: Lake County Historical Society, 2004.

"Tiptonville in 1924." *Lake County News* reprint from June 20, 1924. *Yearbook*. Tiptonville, Tenn: Lake County Historical Society, 2003.

Tri-County News. McKenzie, Tennessee.

Twain, Mark. *Life on the Mississippi*. New York: The Heritage Press, 1944. originally Boston: James R. Osgood & Co., 1883.

Bibliography

Twain, Mark. *Adventures of Huckleberry Finn*. New York: Charles L. Webster & Co., 1885.

Vanderwood, Paul Joseph. *The Night Riders of West Tennessee*. Memphis State University: Masters thesis, 1958.

Vanderwood, Paul J. *Night Riders of Reelfoot Lake*. Memphis: Memphis State University Press, 1969.

Vandiver, Margaret. *Lethal Punishment: Lynchings and Legal Executions in the South*. New Brunswick, New Jersey: Rutgers University Press, 2006.

Walker, Paul E. *Illustrated History of Reelfoot Lake*. Ridgely, Tenn.: self-published, 1929.

Wallis, Michael. *David Crockett: The Lion of the West*. New York: W.W. Norton Co., 2011.

Ward, Andy D., Stanley W. Trimble, Suzette R. Burckhart, and John G. Lyon. *Environmental Hydrology, 3rd Edition*. Boca Raton, FL: CRC Press, 2016.

Warren, Robert Penn. *Night Rider*. New York: Random House, 1939.

Washington, Booker T. *Up from Slavery*. New York: Doubleday, 1901.

Wigdor, Emma. *Early Lake County Churches*. Tiptonville, Tenn: unpublished manuscript in the personal collection of Emily Lewis.

Williams, Bobby Joe. *Mid-South Views the Floods of 1912 and 1913*. Memphis: West Tennessee Historical Society, Vol. 29, 1975.

Wilson, Ealon V. *Life and Ministry of John R. Williams*. Memphis: The Christian Visitor, 1974.

Wolfe, Thomas. *Look Homeward, Angel*. New York: Charles Scribner's Sons, 1929.

"Work, for the Night is Coming." Lyrics by Anna Louisa Walker (Mrs. Harry) Coghill. 1854.

Wyatt-Brown, Bertram. *Southern Honor*. New York: Oxford University Press, 1982.

.

Upper Blue Basin in early Fall, Reelfoot Lake

Illustrations

Illustrations

Illustrations

Illustrations

Illustrations

Illustrations

Illustrations

Illustrations

Index

alcohol, 112.
Alexander, George, 67,
    J.M.,67, William, 29.
automobiles, 32,112,148.
Barr, Tenn., 30.
Bashears, Willis, 109.
Bass, Will, 67.
Bayou de Chein, 8.
Beckham massacre, 16.
Bessie Bend. *See* Kentucky Bend
Bessie, Tenn.,
    31,36,41,58,67,98,134.
Bible, 31,73,99.
biscuits, 59,105,119.
Blytheville, Ark., 11,135.
Bogota, Tenn., 112.
Boyette's Restaurant, 117.
Burdick, J.C., 2,50,54.
Carmack, Edward Ward, 5.
Carroll County, Tenn., 2,18,**22-
30**,36,50,68,74,117.
Cartmell, Robert, 25,75.
Carver, George Washington, 80.
Cates, Clifton, 44.
Cates Landing, Tenn., 31,36,40,
    42,44,58,67,83,91,103
Cedar Grove, Tenn.,
    18,24,27,28,30.
cemeteries, 31,101,138.
children,
    27,38,63,92,94,**97**,105,110
churches, 27,31,75,80,103,104.
civilization,
    32,44,92,106,142,147.
Civil War, American, *See* War
    Between the States
Clemens, Samuel, *See* Mark
    Twain
Cole, R.S., 2,74.

Confederacy,
    15,16,25,26,72,101.
Cook:
    Ann, 23,34.
    Daisy, 98.
    Dee, 25-27,36,69.
    Francis, 26-27.
    George, 25.
    Griffin, 42,66,109,118,123,
        131,137.
    Helen, 97,117,118,126,131.
    Joe (Will's brother), 19.
    Joe (Will's son), 104,117,
        118,127,136.
    John, 2,18,30,31,35,42,43,50,
        59,67-69,103,135
    Joseph, 22-25,27.
    Josie, 135.
    Kathleen, 30,36,66,
        111-113,116,121,148.
    Lambert, 104,117-119,129,
        131,136.
    L.D., 67,108,117,118,
        125,146.
    Libby, 99,104,117,128.
    Malcolm, 44,118,124.
    Pauline, 30,36,66,104,
        111-112,117,120,
        131,138.
    Rachel, 29-30,36,42,44,67,
        97,103,104,111,114,
        116-117.
    R E, 117,118,130,131,136.
    Thomas, 21,23,24.
    Woody (Big), 42,106,109,
        118,122.
    Woody (Little), vii, 84.
cotton farming, 24,27,31,35,**57**,
    72,100,110,134.

Index

Index

Index

trees, 22,27,33,34,48,136.
Truman, President, 136.
truth,79,87,133,142,143,
    145,149.
Twain, Mark, (author), 37,71,91.
twain, mark, (unit of measure),39
Union, 15-16,25-26,67,73-76.
Union City, Tenn., 36.
violence, 11,15-17,31,47,
    82-84,91-93.
Virginia Military Institute, 87.
wagons, 36,62,64,81,98,103.
Walker, Dave, 51-52.
Walker, Henry, 84.
Walnut Street house, 136.

War Between the States, 25,30,
    43,57,67,71,73,76,81,
    87,145.
war crimes, 74-76.
Washington, Booker T., 72,
    76,80.
Weakley County, Tenn., 30,31,
    68.
West Tennessee, **21**.
Williams, John R., 31,103.
Wilson, Woodrow, 42.
women, 23,27,80,92,100,111,
    112,117,143,147.
WW I (World War I), 42,44,65.
WW II (World War II), 44,136.

Black Jack Hollow, Reelfoot Lake,
courtesy of Dr. Robert E. Clendenin, Jr.

Lightning Source UK Ltd.
Milton Keynes UK
UKOW07f0321171017
311117UK00006B/60/P